Performance Dog Nutrition
Optimize Performance with Nutrition

Dr. Jocelynn Jacobs

Library of Congress Cataloging in Publication
Performance Dog Nutrition: Optimize Performance With Nutrition/Jocelynn Jacobs, DVM.

ISBN 0-9759634-0-6
Library of Congress Control Number: 2004098382

The pronouns "he" or "she" have been used in the generic sense to refer to dogs or people of either sex. No bias toward a particular sex is intended.

Many manufacturers secure trademark rights for their products. When Sno Shire Publications is aware of a trademark claim, we print the product name as trademarked or in initial capital letters.

Sno Shire Publications accepts no responsibility for veterinary medical information, suggested treatments, recommendations or vaccinations mentioned herein. This book is meant to supplement the advice and guidance of your veterinarian. We cannot be responsible for unsupervised treatments administered at home. The reader is advised to check with their local, licensed veterinarian before giving medical attention.

All dogs, case studies, pet foods and pet food labels herein are not based on real life cases or real pet foods. They are based on fictional entities.

This and other Sno Shire Publications materials are available to breeders and clubs at special quantity discounts. Write to Customer Service, Sno Shire Publications, 1120 W. Curtis, Sanford, MI 48657.

Credits:
Book design: Kimberly Cloud
Cover design: Deidra Stierly
Photo scans: Ryan Schneider
Proofreading: Christine Zink and Joanne Jacobs
Illustrations: Marcia Schlehr (all drawings and artwork are copywrited)
Front Cover Photos: Kim Booth, Dennis Gulan, Jocelynn Jacobs, and Marsha Standler
Back Cover: Dr. Jocelynn Jacobs with some of her Alaskan malamutes

Printed in the United States of America.

DEDICATION

To my incredibly tolerant husband, Tom Knoll – my guidance counselor and best friend – who supports all my dog hobbies, lets me keep "just one more puppy," and helps train the dogs to keep them in great shape for all the shows…

To my wonderful son, Treven Knoll, who brings me such joy – he helps me keep my priorities straight, and reminds me to stop and smell the dandelions…

To all my dogs (too many to name) who have filled my life with much love, support, and companionship – I can't imagine how different my life would be without you all….

JOCELYNN JACOBS

DONATION PAGE

This page was auctioned at the 2001 Alaskan Malamute Club of America's National Specialty for the Alaskan Malamute Research Foundation. Multiple malamute fanciers donated money to AMRF and dedicated this page to Nancy Russell of Storm Kloud Kennel. Nancy Russell owned the first all AKC registered Alaskan Malamute team to run Alaska's Iditarod in 1994. She also covets some of the best records for weight pulling Alaskan Malamutes. Comments listed below are quoted from her.

"This was the first all AKC registered Alaskan Malamute team to run the Iditarod Trail Race. Seven were AKC conformation champions at the time of the race, and 4 more finished afterward. The purpose was to see if the show dogs I had bred for 30 years had retained their ability to survive and work in their native environment. They averaged 80 miles a day over the roughest part of the course. They enjoyed the cold, had no dehydration, no lactic acid build up, used only half the food we sent, and gained weight during the race. Jamie Nelson, driver of the team, said in the Eskimo villages, the old men brought their grandchildren to see the dogs telling them, 'these are the dogs we used to have.'"

BIS, BISS A/C/Israli Ch. Storm Kloud's
Corner the Market ROM, CGC, WTD, WWPDX

"Cash was the #1 Alaskan Malamute in 1998. He was at the top in national standings for 6 years. Cash won the 1997 AMCA National Specialty Weight Pull where he pulled 3000 lbs three times in his career. At 9 ½ years old, Cash finished the 2001 weight pull season with another 3000 lb pull, and was awarded AMCW's Top Weight Puller in Class B the same day he went Best in Show at the Wisconsin Specialty."

CONTENTS

JOCELYNN JACOBS

THE AUTHOR

At a young age Jocelynn Jacobs, DVM began begging for a dog. Like most parents, her mother and father's response was the typical, "When you grow up, you can have as many dogs as you want!" So, she did just that, making dogs and dog activities the center of her life. Dr. Jacobs obtained her first Arctic breed, a Husky-mix when she was a third year veterinary student at Michigan State University. She and her husband purchased their first AKC registered Alaskan malamute shortly thereafter.

With encouragement from her breeder, Dr. Jacobs began to show dogs in conformation and became infected with the show-bug. To date, she has finished dozens of conformation titles (American and Canadian), and has owner-handled multiple malamutes as specials ranking them top in the country. She is the breeder, owner, and handler of many regional specialty, Alaskan Malamute Club of American (AMCA) National Specialty, sweepstakes, futurity, breed, group winners and group placers. She won Best In Specialty at the AMCA National Specialty in 2003 with "Brewski" (NS-BIS, BISS A/C Ch. Sno Shire's Ice on Tap, WTD) and Best of Opposite Sex at the AMCA National Specialty in 2000 with "Pepzi" (Ch. Sno Shire's Paw Prints on Ice, WTD). Dr. Jacobs was the breeder, owner and handler of both these dogs to their prestigious wins. On occasion, she has been seen in the obedience ring with her malamutes entertaining spectators with their comical antics.

Dr. Jacobs and her husband developed an interest in sled racing and skijoring (cross-country skiing behind a dog in harness) in the early 1990's. Alaskan Malamutes are considered the "Clydesdales" of sled dogs and rarely win sprint races. However, their dog teams are found at the sled races each weekend during the winter, and are quite competitive in skijoring, taking many first place trophies throughout the years. The goal of their breeding program and kennel has been to produce dogs with sound conformation and temperaments that excel on the trail and in the show ring.

After graduating from veterinary school in 1991, Dr. Jacobs worked as a small animal practitioner. Over the years, as her involvement in dog sports progressed, feeding to optimize her dogs' performance became top of mind – she realized nutrition was the key to peak performance both in the ring and on the trail. She was offered and took a position with a leading pet food company to enhance her knowledge and understanding of canine nutrition. During those years, reproduction and performance nutrition were her areas of interest because of her background in breeding, showing, and sled racing.

The birth of her son brought Dr. Jacobs back to private practice a few years later, and she owns her own veterinary hospital called Countryside Animal Health Center, LLC in Freeland, Michigan. As a practitioner, she counsels clients on nutrition since she considers it of utmost importance in disease management and treatment. Besides working with her general clientele, she also enjoys working with breeders and performance dog owners doing reproduction work and genetic counseling.

As an active member of the AMCA, Dr. Jacobs has been very involved with health and genetic issues and research. Some of the projects she has been involved in include DNA testing for chondrodysplasia, coat funk (a type of follicle dysplasia found in double-coated breeds) and cataracts.

Dr. Jacobs has been writing articles for dog enthusiasts since 1990. Articles written by her are found in many publications including the *Eukanuba Breeder News* where she not only contributes as an author but also is an editor. With this book, Dr. Jacobs will share practical information about canine nutrition – clearing up some mis-conceptions and give good solid nutritional philosophies – to help dog enthusiasts feed their dogs to optimize their potential. This is her first book in publication.

JOCELYNN JACOBS

ACKNOWLEDGEMENTS

Whew…where do I begin? First I want to thank Christine Zink, author of *Peak Performance: Coaching the Canine Athlete*, for encouraging me to write this book. She gave me great ideas of how to organize the book and provided wonderful insight on my writing style. Thank you, Chris. I really appreciate all your help and encouragement.

Secondly, this book would not be in print today without the help of Kimberly Cloud who did the computer work and layout of the book and photos. It was a long haul for both of us, but her past experience in the printing industry was an incredible asset to make this book look as good as we could make it. She has a wonderful eye for quality of photos and layout ideas. Thank you, Kimberly, and as I have said at least 100 times before this, I couldn't have done this without you!

I want to list a few people and groups that also helped make this book a possibility. Ryan Schneider from Jirehnet Services for scanning and working with Kimberly on the photos; Joanne Jacobs and Margaret Marks for reading through one of the first drafts to make sure it was in a format that was easy to read; again to Margaret for setting up the photo shoot of people in her agility class and allowing me to take photos of her dog, Mick, for herding shots; Joe Fusco who encouraged me to print the book myself and offered all his advice; and finally to all the people (too many to list) who either allowed me to take photos of their dogs or gave me great photos to include in this book. Thanks to all – a piece of each of you is found in this book!

INTRODUCTION

For hundreds of years man has had a unique relationship with the domestic canine. Originally dogs were kept and trained to make the lives of man easier. Dogs were trained for hunting, herding, transportation, and protection. As years passed, their role changed as tools and machines were invented to take their place, however, dogs continue to play an important role in our lives. The modernized man no longer has to hunt to eat, but dogs hunt for sport in field trials. Sled dogs were once mandatory for transportation for those living in Alaska, Canada, and other countries, but with the emergence of snowmobiles, dog sledding now is a hobby or recreational sport for mushers.

As dogs roles have changed from necessity to sport, we have genetically selected them to better meet our needs. Competition has been an effective tool in altering canine structure and performance. Evaluating breeding programs, bloodlines, training methods, and nutrition are top of mind for owners hoping to enhance their dog's performance and workability. Many breeders are, in essence, helping to preserve their dogs' heritage and building upon deep-seeded instincts to improve the quality of their breed.

Racing sled dogs are a perfect example of how we have altered a group of dogs turning them into speedy racing machines. In the 1900's, most sled dogs ran an average of 5 miles per hour. Today many sprint racing dogs can run over

20 miles per hour! Mushers bred older arctic breeds such as the Alaskan Malamute or Siberian Husky to hounds and sporting dogs that in turn increased endurance and speed. These dogs are called Alaskan Huskies, and although not recognized by the American and Canadian Kennel Club, they are known as speed demons of the sled trails. These dogs, being selectively bred as high-speed racers, have high metabolic rates paralleling their speed. While the average 50 pound house dog may only require 1,000 kilocalories, an average active hunting dog of the same weight may require 1,600 kilocalories a day. In comparison, an Alaskan Huskies running the Iditarod sled dog race can require up to 10,000 kilocalories a day to meet their energy needs and maintain body condition! So it is easy to see how genetic alteration of type and function affects our dogs' metabolic needs.

Hunting, herding, sledding, and protecting are not the only activities dogs participate in. There has been an explosion of new performance events for dogs in the recent years. In addition to conformation and obedience, there now are agility trials, lure coursing competitions, earth dog events, weight pulls, disc catching, and many more ways dogs and handlers demonstrate their athletic ability through competition.

Agility is one of the hottest new sports for dogs. In agility, dogs jump over jumps, run through tunnels, and balance on teeter-totters as quickly as possible, and amazingly enough, without a leash! These dogs are guided through a maze of obstacles with just hand signals and voice commands of their owners. Both purebred and mixed breed dogs can participate. Winners and title-holders are those dogs that not only have the brains and speed, but

are kept in top physical and mental condition for quick maneuvering.

If you enjoy dog sports, and want your dog to reach their peak performance potential through nutrition, this book is for you! In these pages, you will find important nutritional information that will help improve your dog's strength and endurance whether your dog is a hunting or tracking dog running in the field and marsh all day, herding dog gathering sheep during a herding trial, sled dog running long distance races, agility dog racing through obstacle courses, or conformation dog competing on the campaign trail.

JOCELYNN JACOBS

JOCELYNN JACOBS

CHAPTER 1

How Food is Digested

What you will know after reading this chapter:

· What happens to food after it is swallowed

· How food gets transported through the body

· How dog food gets transformed into usable nutrients

· How long it takes for food to go through the entire digestive track

· What the pancreas and liver do

· How performance dogs compare to non-working dogs in their digestive requirements

Have you ever wondered how a couple scoops of dog food provides all the energy and nutrients your dog needs for a full day of work? The transformation of food into individual nutrients and energy is complex, but fortunately, your dog's body does it with ease. Each organ in their digestive tract has a specific job, breaking down large chunks of meat or cups of dog food into everything they need to function. As long as food is ingested and the organs are doing their job, your performance dog can train, compete, and perform to the best of their ability.

ROLE OF THE DIGESTIVE TRACT

There are two major functions of the digestive tract: digestion and absorption. Digestion is the *degradation* (breakdown) of food into its components. Absorption is the uptake of nutrients into circulation. Most vitamins and minerals do not require digestion, however, some are chemically altered before they are absorbed and used by the body. Protein, fats, and carbohydrates all require digestion prior to absorption. Proteins must be broken into single amino acids (the building blocks of protein) or peptides (a few amino acids linked together). Fats are broken down into glycerol, free fatty acids, and some mono- or diglycerides. And complex carbohydrates are broken into the simple sugars glucose, fructose, and galactose prior to absorption.

Breaking down proteins, fats, and carbohydrates into smaller, absorbable units is accomplished mechanically, chemically, and microbially (bacterial degradation). The mouth mechanically breaks down food into smaller pieces, increasing the surface area so chemical digestion can take place. The stomach and intestines chemically work on the food, secreting enzymes and acids to break down proteins and fats into smaller sub-units. Bacteria throughout the digestive tract microbially work on the food. Bacteria use some sub-units for their own nutrition, and produce by-products that supply energy and nourishment for your dog.

The dog's digestive tract is controlled by voluntary and involuntary actions. Chewing and swallowing are examples of voluntary actions – the dog consciously controls these actions. Once food is swallowed, involuntary actions take over. The dog no longer has conscious control of when food goes from the stomach to the intestines or how fast it travels through the intestines. Regaining voluntary control doesn't occur until they defecate stool. In most instances, a healthy dog can delay defecation until the right time and place arises. During bouts of diarrhea, however, having voluntary control may be over-ridden by involuntary actions of rapidly moving material in the intestines.

LENGTH AND TRANSIT TIME

The dog's digestive tract is approximately 4 to 5 times the total body length of the dog. So if your dog is 20 inches from brisket to rump, his digestive tract is approximately 80 to 100 inches in length. A long digestive tract means longer transit time for food and more efficient digestion. In the dog, it takes about 22 hours for food to travel from the mouth to the colon – this provides ample time for digestion and absorption to take place.

In the dog, the small and large intestines have a very large surface area. The small intestine's lining is covered by small finger-like projections called *villi* that increase the surface area seven-fold, and allow for maximum absorption of nutrients.

The type of diet, frequency of feeding, outside temperature, pregnancy, exercise, stress, and age all affect transit and absorption time – each should be considered when feeding a performance dog. Poor quality foods (with poorly

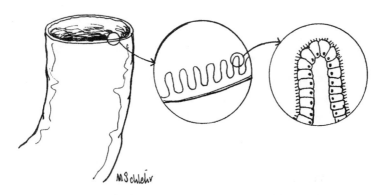

Cross section of the intestine with a close up of the villi (finger-like projections) and cells of the villi lining the intestines enhancing the absorptive capacity.

digestible nutrients) move through the intestines faster which means fewer nutrients are properly digested and absorbed.

Extreme temperatures can also affect transit time. In warm temperatures, intestines may have quicker transit times, but in an overheated dog, the intestines may shut down to divert energy for cooling your dog rather than absorbing nutrients. In extremely cold temperatures intestinal speed may slow conserving energy to keep your dog warm.

In late term pregnancy, dogs have increased intestinal transit times primarily because there is little room in the abdomen for a full stomach, full intestines, *and* puppies.

Factor	Increase or decrease intestinal speed
Poor quality food	Increase
Frequent feedings	Increase
Pregnancy	Increase
Exercise	Increase
Young age	Increase
Stress	Increase
Cold temperatures	Increase
Old age	Increase or Decrease
Hot temperatures	Increase or Decrease
Once daily feeding	Decrease

Exercise and stress will increase intestinal transit time. Thus, it is important to rest working and performance dogs regularly so the digestive tract has time to absorb nutrients for the next bout of exercise.

Age also influences transit time and nutrient absorption rates. Young puppies and active youngsters often have quick intestinal speeds preventing proper absorption of nutrients. This is one good reason to feed puppies multiple small meals through the day. Senior dogs may have either increased or decreased transit times depending on the type of food they are fed. Older dogs, just as in older humans, often have poorer nutrient absorption causing them to be thin with poor muscle tone. Specifically designed senior diets can be beneficial to keeping them in proper body condition and weight.

ORGANS OF THE DIGESTIVE TRACT

There are six major organs in the canine digestive tract: mouth, esophagus, stomach, small intestine, large intestine, and rectum/anus.

The Mouth

The mouth's primary function is mechanical in nature – ripping, grinding, and chewing. Dogs have 42 teeth (compared to only 30 in the cat). The incisors and premolars of the dog are used for ripping and tearing flesh away from a

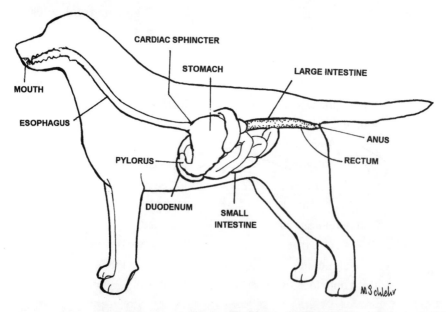

Organs of the Canine Digestive System

carcass. Dogs have very large 4th premolars and 1st molars that are used for grinding flesh or chewing dog food kibble. The act of chewing is not as important in dogs as it is in humans or herbivores (rabbits, cows, goats, and horses). Humans and herbivores eat plants, vegetables, and fruits which have coatings of tough, undigestible cellulose. Chewing is important for breaking down cellulose to release nutrients from these foods. Most domesticated dogs eat commercially produced kibble or canned food, and little chewing is required. However, large back premolars and molars are helpful when chewing on bones, rawhide, cow hooves, and other doggie delicacies.

Another important function of the mouth is producing saliva. Saliva is secreted by salivary glands when food is present. In some cases, even anticipating food results in its secretion.

Saliva is 99% water. The remaining 1% is made up of mucus, inorganic salts, and enzymes. Of these three components, mucus is the most important to coat food particles to aid in swallowing. Saliva also helps the chewing process by allowing food to move easily from one side of the mouth to the other to clump, aiding in pulverization.

Just as in humans, dogs have taste buds on their tongues. They allow the dog to enjoy their food, encouraging them to eat. During times of high stress or competition, performance dogs sometimes may lose their interest in eating. Increasing the palatability (tastiness) of their food will encourage them to eat

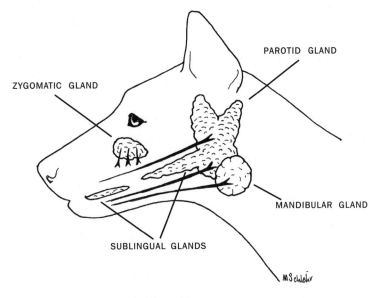

Salivary Glands of the Dog

more. Dogs appear to be more tempted by foods high in fat, while humans enjoy foods higher in salt and sugar.

The Esophagus

The esophagus is a long muscular, tubular organ that transports food from the mouth to the stomach. Food spends very little time in the esophagus – only a few seconds. The esophagus does not excrete any enzymes to aid in digestion. Involuntary wave-like motion called *peristalsis* pushes food toward the stomach. At the end of the esophagus, there is an opening to the stomach called the *cardiac sphincter* (a valve-like structure). This sphincter is normally closed, but when food reaches it, it relaxes and opens to allow food to enter the stomach.

Normally food only goes in one direction in the esophagus – toward the stomach. However, when a dog vomits, the direction is reversed. Two organs control whether vomiting is allowed to occur – the stomach and the brain. The stomach can permit vomiting when something is irritating its lining, such as toxic chemicals, non-digestible toys, or over-production of stomach acids. When this happens, a reflex is stimulated, the cardiac sphincter is opened, and material from the stomach is push up the esophagus to the mouth. The brain can also control vomiting. Motion sickness is a good example of when the brain stimulates vomiting. In humans, certain visual stimuli can also stimulate the vomiting reflex.

The Stomach

Contrary to what most people think, the stomach does not absorb nutrients. Its main function is as a holding and mixing tank, preparing food for transport into the intestines where absorption takes place. The stomach adds many digestive juices aiding in degradation. Gastric juices initiate protein digestion; assist in

---

5 Functions of the Stomach:

1. Temporary food storage

2. Secretion of enzymes and acid for digestion

3. Mixing of food

4. Movement of food to the small intestine

5. Control of food flow

---

intestinal absorption of calcium, vitamin B12, and iron; and help maintain viability of normal intestinal bacteria.

Pepsinogen (an enzyme) and hydrochloric acid (HCl) are produced by the lining of the stomach and mix with stomach contents. HCl alters pepsinogen into pepsin which breaks protein into amino acids and peptides. Protein takes

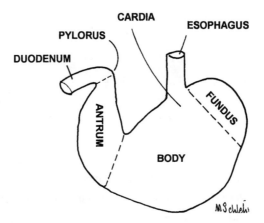

The Canine Stomach

longer to digest than fats or carbohydrates, so the stomach initiates protein digestion with pepsin, and the intestines complete the process. Diets higher in animal protein causes more pepsin to be produced compared to diets higher in plant protein. This is because animal protein has higher levels of collagen. Once food moves into the intestines, pepsin becomes inactivated, and protein is broken down through other digestive mechanisms.

The stomach also secretes mucus. This gel-like material lines the stomach protecting it from hydrochloride acid and stomach enzymes. Mucus is also important for healing stomach ulcers and prevents occurrence of ulcers both in the stomach and upper intestine.

The brain has significant control on the secretion of gastric juices and stomach mixing. Smelling or anticipating food produces secretion of gastric juices into the stomach even when food is not present. The brain also stimulates secretion of gastric juices into the

What is the role of the pancreas in digestion?

The pancreas produces additional digestive enzymes. There are small ducts (tubes) connecting the pancreas to the small intestine in the duodenum where enzymes are released to mix with chyme. The pancreatic enzymes include proteases that break protein down into amino acids or peptides (short chains of amino acids), lipases that break down fats, and amylases that break down starches or carbohydrates. The pancreas also releases hormones such as insulin that encourages the uptake of glucose by cells throughout the body.

stomach during times of stress, fear, or anxiety. This occurs via stimulation of the sympathetic nervous system. This causes two problems for performance dogs. First, excess gastric juice in the absence of food causes irritation to the stomach lining and vomiting results. Young dogs new to performance activities commonly suffer from this. Stress of traveling and anxiety surrounding the event results in excess gastric juice formation, and prior to the event, the dog may vomit. Simply offering a dog biscuit prior to the event may help absorb gastric juices and promote its movement into the small intestine.

The second problem occurs with dogs being heavily trained or campaigned. Chronic production of excess gastric juices from stress erodes the lining of the stomach forming ulcers. Again, offering small dog treats during training, exercise, or prior to an event helps absorb excess enzymes and acids, and moves them on to the neutral pH environment of the intestine. Heavily trained and campaigned dogs should have ample time off and rest to decrease stress and excess gastric juice production.

Once food is mixed with gastric juices in the stomach, it forms a semi-liquid material called **chyme**. Movement of ingesta to the small intestine can not take place until chyme has formed. The size of the meal fed can determine how quickly food becomes chyme. In general, the larger the meal, the longer it takes to form chyme, and the slower the stomach contents move into the intestines. Smaller meals form chyme quicker and exit the stomach faster. This is an important point to consider for the performance dog. If your dog needs to be fed before an event but you do not want them to have a full stomach making them sluggish, feed a small meal rather than a large one. Additionally, diets made with poor-quality proteins and poor digestibility take longer to make into chyme which delays stomach emptying. Performance dogs should only be fed diets with highly digestible proteins and nutrients commonly found in premium performance dog foods.

Diets high in fat can also cause delayed stomach emptying. High fat diets, however, are important when feeding the performance dog for adequate energy requirements – thus a conflict appears to exist. However, by feeding multiple *small* meals of diets higher in fat to your canine athletes, you can meet their both energy and nutrient needs and at the same time promote ideal stomach emptying rates.

> ### Does the liver play a part in digestion of food?
>
> Yes. It produces *bile* which is stored in the gallbladder. When food is present the gallbladder secretes bile into the small intestine via a duct. Bile breaks down fats and activates certain enzymes to further aid in digestion.

The valve that separates the stomach and small intestine is called the *pyloric sphincter.* It opens based on the following:

1. The amount of distention (swelling) of the stomach – the more distended the stomach, the more quickly it will open.
2. The degree of distention of the duodenum (the first section of the small intestine) — if the duodenum is too full, it will not open.
3. The pH of the duodenal chyme – if the pH is too low, it will not open.
4. Irritation to the lining of the duodenum – if the lining is irritated, the sphincter will not open as frequently.
5. The presence of small enough particles in the chyme – if large particles remain in the chyme, the pyloric sphincter will not open. This encourages the stomach to continue to mix and breakdown the food.

The Small Intestine

Without a doubt, the small intestine is the most important part of the entire digestive tract. It is where the majority of digestion and absorption of nutrients occurs in the dog. The small intestine is called "small" because of its diameter, not its length. In fact, the small intestine is the longest part of the digestive tract allowing for maximum digestion and absorption to take place.

The small intestine has three sections: the duodenum (the first section, closest to the stomach), the jejunum (the middle section), and the ileum (the end section just before the large intestine).

The small intestine furthers digestion through mechanical and chemical needs. It is lined by smooth muscles that produce wave-like contractions to mix chyme. It also releases several enzymes that digest fats, carbohydrates, and proteins.

The small intestine almost completely breaks down protein, fat, and carbohydrates. The end results are amino acids and peptides (from protein digestion), free fatty acids (from

MARSHA STANDLER

fat digestion), and glucose (from carbohydrate digestion). These end products are then absorbed into the blood stream and distributed to other organs and tissues of the body.

The lining of the small intestine has a huge surface area – about 1 square mile in the average 40 lb dog! Finger like projections called villi cover the lining of the small intestine, and the villi have specialized absorptive cells called **entrocytes.** These cells have a very short life span – they only live 2 or 3 days before they die and are sloughed into the lumen (the passageway of the intestines) to pass out with feces. The growth and turnover of these cells is important. Viruses, bacteria, or toxins that damage enterocytes or prevent their regrowth can seriously affect nutrient absorption. Dogs infected with intestinal viruses such as canine parvovirus (CPV) or corona virus have significant damage occur to their intestinal lining. This hampers nutrient digestion and absorption, and the dogs lose weight quickly.

Nutrients are absorbed by cells lining the small intestine and the blood stream by two methods. The first method is called **passive diffusion** where nutrients move from the lumen passively into the cells or bloodstream. The second method is **active transport**, where energy is used to transport nutrients from the lumen to the cells and blood vessels. These processes can be compared to a canoe on water. When the canoe floats with the current it is similar to passive diffusion – the canoe is going with the flow of the river. However, when you paddle up stream against the current it is similar to active transport since it take energy to get to the desired location.

In addition to proteins, fats and carbohydrates, vitamins and minerals are also absorbed by the small and large intestines. How much is absorbed depends

My dog passes a lot of gas. What is causing this?

If you are feeding a poor quality dog food, excess bacterial fermentation will produce excess gas formation. If you are feeding a high quality, highly digestible dog food and still have excessive gas production, then look at the fiber source. Different dogs respond differently to fiber sources. Just like some humans can't eat beans or onions without getting gassy, certain fiber sources have similar effects on certain dogs. Some companies use poorly digestible fiber sources such as cellulose or peanut hulls – these diets may produce excess gas. Each dog's ability to digest certain fiber sources is different, and it may be as easy as finding the right dog food with the right fiber source to decrease his gas production. There also are some nutritional supplements in pet stores that boast they will reduce gas production. You might want to try some of these to see if they help.

on the body's requirement for that mineral or vitamin and the form the vitamin or mineral is present in. **Fat soluble vitamins**, such as A, D, E, and K, require fat to be present in food for proper absorption. **Water soluble vitamins** B and C are usually absorbed by passive diffusion into the blood stream. Vitamin B12 is an exception to this rule since its uptake requires binding to a protein known as the **intrinsic factor** before it can be absorbed.

The Large Intestine

Digesta from the small intestines passes to the large intestine via the **ileo-cecal valve**. The large intestine is wider in diameter than the small intestine, but it is fairly short in length. It also is relatively straight, unlike the coiled small intestine. It has three sections: the ascending colon, the transverse colon, and the descending colon named according to the direction of flow. The digesta first

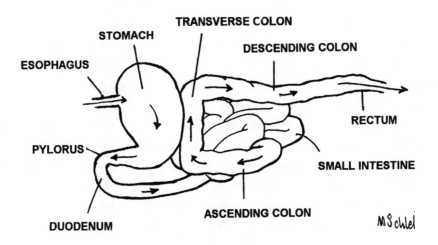

Flow of Digesta in the Canine Gastrointestinal Tract

flows in the direction of the dog's head in the ascending colon, then across the body from right to left in the transverse colon, then turns toward the rectum in the descending colon.

The lining of the large intestine is very different from that of the small intestine. It has a flat surface with no finger-like projections or villi. It does, however, have many glands which secrete fluids to lubricate the waste material (feces) so they can pass out easily.

The primary function of the large intestine is to absorb water and electrolytes from the semi-liquid material that leaves the small intestine. This prevents the dog from losing water and firms the stool. In contrast to the rapid flow of material in the small intestine, the movement of material through the large intestine is very slow and non-propulsive. Fecal material in the large intestines can be stored for quite a while until an appropriate opportunity to defecate arises.

Another important phenomenon that occurs in the large intestine is **bacterial fermentation**. Large colonies of beneficial bacteria live in the large intestine and aid in digestion of nutrients such as certain proteins, some carbohydrates, and fiber.

Bacteria living in the intestine can ferment (break down) certain types of fibers. Different types of fibers have differing abilities to ferment. When intestinal bacteria break down fiber through fermentation, they produce by-products called short-chain fatty acids that support the health of the lining of the intestine. This improves the health of the intestinal lining allowing better absorption. Thus fiber can be very important in keeping your dog's intestinal tract healthy (see Chapter 8 for additional information on fiber).

Bacterial fermentation in the large intestine is what creates the characteristic color and smell to the stool. Additionally, when bacteria break down fecal material, gas is produced as a by-product. Hydrogen, carbon dioxide, nitrogen, and methane gases are the gases released. Technically this is referred to as *flatulence* or more commonly "passing gas." Poorly digestible foods and diets high in certain types of carbohydrates such as soybeans are not completely digested and absorbed by the small intestine. They then end up in the large intestine where bacterial fermentation occurs, and the end result is excess flatulence.

Stool in the large intestine stretches the wall of the intestines and stimulates defecation. The internal and external anal sphincters open and fecal material is released. The brain has some control over the opening of the anal sphincters. At times, however, the reflex to defecate may be too great for the brain to over-ride and stool is release involuntarily as in the case of diarrhea.

APPLICATION TO PERFORMANCE DOGS

As trainers and handlers of performance dogs, it is important to monitor the quality and amount of stool your dog produces. The stool can provide important information about they quality of the food being fed, such as:

1. **How digestible is the dog's food?** In general, excess amounts of stool suggest that the dog's food may not be highly digestible. Highly digestible foods produce smaller amounts of fecal matter on a daily basis.

2. **Is the large intestine absorbing the proper amount of water?** Diarrhea (caused by excess water in the stool) can result from improper resorption of water in the large intestines, perhaps because of damage from viral or bacterial infections or parasites. Diarrhea can also be caused by an infection or malabsorption condition of the small intestines.

3. **Is there excess gas formation?** Poorly digestible foods commonly produce excess gas. However, other things such as bacterial or viral infections of the intestinal lining, or damaged caused by parasites can also affect whether nutrients are absorbed in the small intestines. If the lining of the small intestine is damaged or not working properly, nutrients may be moved to the large intestine where bacterial fermentation produces excessive gas.

Evaluating what comes out of your dog can give you quite a bit of information about the food that is going in. Get in the habit of regularly checking stool amount and quality since it is an important part of taking good care of your performance dog.

MARSHA STANDLER

Case File: Isaac and the mysterious missing toy

A 13 month old Alaskan Malamute, named Isaac, was producing what looked like vomited blood in his kennel – about four or five times per week. There was never any food in it, and it was not stool because the owner would watch him have normal stools each day while out playing. He was eating his food well and growing.

Isaac was in a middle kennel with the alpha male kenneled to his right and another large, but not extremely dominate male to his left. He would play and act completely normal, but was intimated by the alpha male on his right. According to his owner, there were no missing toys from his kennel. His physical examination, including an abdominal palpation, was normal.

Concerned Isaac may have been developing an ulcer because of the alpha dog, he was started on sucralfate (an ulcer medication) and moved to another kennel. This decreased the number of bloody vomit piles over the weeks, but never eliminated the problem.

Over the weeks, Isaac began to eat his meals slower (Malamutes usually inhale their food, never chew), and lose weight. Eventually one morning he stopped eating all together. He had a temperature of 107°, and now a hard mass in his intestines could be felt on palpation.

An x-ray revealed a small, dense mass in the small intestines. Emergency surgery was performed and a piece of hard chew toy was found in the intestines about 15 inches

Page 1

from the stomach. There were sharp edges all around this toy which was causing irritation to his stomach producing bloody vomit. Eventually the toy passed into the intestines where it became lodged.

Isaac recovered well after surgery and was back on the sled team within a couple months!

Page 2

CHAPTER 2

Commercial and Homemade Diets

What you will know after reading this chapter:

·   How dry dog foods are manufactured

·   Whether the manufacturing process alters nutrient profiles

·   Advantages of dry and canned formulations

·   Whether all commercial dog foods the same basic quality

·   How preservatives work and which are better

·   What basic types of homemade diets are available

·   Some points to evaluate when considering a homemade diet

·   How supplementation of certain raw ingredients may be
    helpful in specific performance dog situations

When it comes to feeding your performance dog you have three choices – feed commercial dog food, make your own diet, or feed a combination of the two. There are advantages and disadvantages to each option which warrants their discussion. This chapter takes an in-depth look of different diets available and how they can be best used when feeding a performance dog.

HISTORY OF DOG FOOD

Until the mid 1800's, all dogs were fed homemade diets in the form of left-over scraps since no commercially prepared foods were available. It wasn't until 1860, James Spratt, an American living in London, produced and introduced the first commercially prepared dog food in a biscuit form.

Throughout the early 1900's, others saw the success Spratt was having in selling his dog food, and shortly afterward, both canned and dry dog food became available. Most dog foods of this era were made of left-over ingredients from human food processing. Most contained very high levels of cereals and grains.

In the 1950's, the extrusion process was developed. This revolutionized the manufacturing of commercially available dry dog food – making dog foods easier to produce and more palatable than previous diets. With extrusion all ingredients are mixed together, cooked under high temperatures, and pushed through a die with a rotating knife to cut the food into desired shapes and size. The extrusion process results in rapid cooking of the starches in food that enhances digestibility and taste. Because dogs liked the extruded foods better than those marketed by Spratt and other manufacturers, their popularity increased.

COMMERCIAL DIETS

Dry Dog Food

Dry dog food is the most commonly purchased food today. Compared to canned or semi-moist foods, dog owners find it more economical and easily stored. For owners of large breeding and working kennels, dry food is preferred since large quantities are easily purchased at one time, and it has a reasonably long shelf-life when stored under proper conditions. Some owners like dry dog foods because they feel they can leave food in their pet's bowl through the day without worry about spoilage or drying of the product.

Dry dog food typically has a caloric density between 3,000 and 4,500 kilocalories (kcal) of metabolizable energy (ME) per kilogram (kg). On a dry matter basis it is between 1,300 and 2,000 kcal/pound. Some performance dog foods are more calorically dense than others and may exceed 4,500kcal/kg. In general, dry dog foods have a higher caloric density than canned or semi-moist foods. Primarily this is because both canned and semi-moist foods have higher water content. Therefore dry dog foods generally have more calories in a cup than does a cup of canned food. This means eating 1 cup of dry food usually provides more calories (i.e. more calorically dense) than 1 cup of canned food.

Most canned and semi-moist foods are more palatable than dry dog foods. This is especially true when feeding a dry food that is low in fat, has poor quality ingredients, or derives most of its protein from plant sources rather than animal. Most premium performance dry dog foods are higher in animal protein and fat content, and generally have better palatability.

The Extrusion Process

All dry dog foods today are produced using the extrusion process. Extruders are machines used in this process. They mix ingredients together to form a dough which is cooked under high pressures and temperatures that kills and aids in prevent of bacteria and fungus growth. The dough moves very quickly through the extruder and cooking occurs very rapidly – usually within 20 to 60 seconds. When mixed and cooked dough reaches the end of the extruder, it is forced through a small opening and a rotating knife cuts the food into desired shapes and sizes forming kibbles. After the kibbles cool and dry, some companies will spray a coating of fat on them to further enhance palatability. The drying process reduces the total moisture content of most dry dog foods to 6 - 10 %.

Some manufacturers of poor-quality, low priced dry foods have ingredients that inherently have very low digestibility and nutrient availability. Thus, during the extrusion process, additional nutrients are lost. It always is worth it in the long run to buy premium quality dry dog foods from companies with reputations of producing high quality diets.

Canned Dog Food

There are two types of canned dog foods on the market today. The first type is labeled ***nutritionally complete and balanced*** for all the vitamins, minerals, and nutrients recommended by nutritional guidelines for dogs. This type of canned food contains mixtures of muscle meats, poultry, and fish by-products, cereal grains, texturized vegetable proteins, vitamins, and minerals. These foods can be used as the sole source of nutrients for a dog without worry of nutritional deficiencies.

The second type of canned food on the market is commonly referred to as ***canned meat products***. This type of canned food is not formulated to be nutritionally complete and balanced. Rather it is used as a supplement to enhance the flavor or increase the amount of protein or fat in a diet. Most owners add this type of canned food in small amounts to a nutritionally balanced dry dog food.

Canned dog food has a very high water content. Most contain about 75% water. Because of the high water content, the concentration of nutrients in canned foods, in general, is less than dry foods. Fat content of canned food is usually higher at 20-32% compared to the fat content of most dry dog foods at 20-25% on a dry matter basis. Most canned dog foods have a relatively small amount of digestible carbohydrates in them compared to dry foods. These two things alone help to increase its flavor.

Canned foods are usually more expensive to feed than dry dog foods. This is not as much of a concern for smaller breeds of dogs who only need to be fed ½ can of food a day to meet their nutrient requirements. But in large breed dogs, such as Komondors, because of how dilute canned food is, it may require over a half dozen cans a day to meet their nutritional needs! That can get very expensive very quickly.

Does the extrusion process damage essential vitamins and nutrients in dry dog foods?

The heating process through extrusion can result in minor losses of some nutrients, so most premium quality dog food manufacturers compensate for them. They compare vitamin, mineral, and nutrient content of the food before and after processing, and accordingly make changes and additions to the initial formulations to make up for processing losses. This ensures that their ingredient profiles and digestibility stay high.

The Canned Food Processing Technique

Meat, fat ingredients, and water are blended together when making canned food. Then dry ingredients such as vitamins and minerals and other nutrient components are added to the mixture and heated. After heating, the food is put into cans on a conveyor belt, sealed with double seams, washed, and identification coded. They then are immediately pressured cooked – a process called *retorting*. Typically cans are cooked at 250° Celsius for 1 hour, although temperatures and times can vary with the product and can size. After retorting, the cans are cooled and checked for seal integrity.

Another advantage to canned foods is they usually have an relatively long shelf-life (most have the shelf life of 2 years). Canned food is cooked under high pressures and temperatures and sealed tightly for longer storage times.

The texture of canned foods is very appealing to most dogs. This coupled with the high palatability helps make this form of food good for highly stressed, sick, or debilitated dogs.

Semi-Moist Dog Foods

Semi-moist dog foods have less water content that canned foods but higher than dry dog foods. The typical water content is 15 - 30%. They are softer in texture than dry dog foods which contributes to their increased acceptance among most dogs. Prevention of spoilage or contamination is a major concern with semi-moist foods. Most companies use *humectants* such glycerol, corn syrup, or simple sugars which bind water molecules in the food making it harder for invading bacteria to affect them. Prevention of yeasts and molds is accomplished by the addition of potassium sorbate and small amount of organic acids to decrease the pH of semi-moist foods to inhibit bacterial growth.

Because of the high content of simple sugars in semi-moist foods, the flavor and digestibility is enhanced. These foods also contain a lower fat level compared to canned or dry dog food, usually ranging between 8 - 14% on a dry matter basis. This lowers the caloric concentration, and for that reason, is not ideal for most performance dogs that require high numbers of calories per day to meet their energy needs.

My Border Collie so busy all the time, he doesn't seem to want to take the time to eat! What can I do to ensure he gets the nutrients he needs, and make it tasty enough that he will want to take time to eat?

Mixing a high quality, premium performance dry dog food with a half a can of high quality canned food may do the trick. Dry dog food will have the proper caloric density to assure he is getting the calories and nutrients he needs while the canned food will help to increase palatability. Feeding him all canned food isn't ideal because he will have to eat many more cups of canned food than dry to make up for the caloric density difference. That will make him feel too full to finish the required amount to get the nutrients he needs.

KIMBERLY CLOUD

Instead, semi-moist foods more effectively are used to add flavor to dry dog foods.

THE QUALITY RANGE

There are many different commercial dog foods on the market today. They range from poor quality, low-priced, generic foods all the way up to high quality, expensive, premium pet foods. The wide range in quality reflects the wide range of owner demands. Some people pick foods based strictly on lowest price. Some people pick foods based on how much their dog seems to enjoy it. To most performance dog owners, while cost is a factor, a food's ability to enhance performance is given highest priority.

For optimal performance, it is essential to feed a food that meets your dog's specific nutritional requirements. In general, there are three types of commercial dog foods available. These are *premium*, *private label*, and *generic commercial* dog foods.

Premium Commercial Dog Food

Premium dog foods are those developed with optimal nutrition and the most recent research considered in the formulation. They have high quality, highly digestible ingredients, such as animal protein and fats, and have consistent ingredients bag to bag otherwise known as fixed formulations. Quality control of premium foods' manufacture process is highly tuned, and concern about producing the highest quality product possible is a priority. Companies of premium dog foods use feeding trials to assure their product's quality meets governmental recommendations, and base their formulation on current research on canine nutrition. They commonly have specific diets to meet specific needs of groups of dogs whether they are performance dogs, puppies, adults, or dogs with disease conditions requiring special blends of ingredients to meet specific health requirements.

People who frequently purchase premium foods are companion animal owners, hobbyists, and professional trainers – those very concerned with giving their dog the best food possible for its activity and life-style. Premium dog foods are usually nutrient dense – that is, a smaller amount of food needs to be fed because the caloric concentration is high and ingredients are highly digestible. In general, premium foods cost more, but since less has to be fed to maintain the nutritional status of the dog, the cost per serving is often comparable to other brands of dog food.

Private Label Dog Foods

Private label foods are those that carry a store or a chain name. Private label foods are manufactured by an independent contractor, and then a private label is put on the product. Most private label foods have cost top of mind. In general, these companies want to manufacture a product that has minimal ingredient cost so the overall cost to the consumer is lower than premium foods. Lower cost ingredients means lesser quality ingredients and lower digestibility. Companies who manufacture and sell these foods may try to "clone" a higher quality product – they may imitate the packaging, bag colors, or designs, name, and/or ingredient lists of premium foods. They may have the same top three or four ingredients of the labels of premium foods, but when further evaluated these ingredients are not the same quality of those found in premium brands (See Chapter 3). Additionally, many private labeled foods do not use feeding trials to assure their product meets governmental and nutrient needs of dogs.

Generic Dog Foods

Generic dog foods may or may not carry a brand or easily recognizable name. Some large pet food companies may have lines of products that are more generic in nature, while having other lines of foods that are high quality. However, the majority of companies that produce generic dog foods only have one line of food targeting the customer that is price conscious. Generic dog foods are usually very low-priced. To offer a low price to the consumer, lesser quality ingredients are used that have lower nutrient availability for the dog. These foods may also lose more nutrients through the extrusion process. Additionally, generic dog foods do not have fixed formulations – that is from bag to bag, the percentage of certain ingredients may changed based on market availability and price. Because the ingredients generally are poorer quality, the palatability of the food is not as good. These foods frequently use flavor enhancers such as garlic or salt may be used to make the product more appealing.

PRESERVATIVES

One of the major concerns facing all pet food manufacturers is safety of their product. A dog food must be able to be both nutritious and safe for consumption throughout its designated shelf life. For most dry dog foods, that shelf life is one year. Preventing bacterial contamination and breakdown of nutrients is important to ensure the food is as good the first day it was manufactured all the way to the "best used by" date listed on the packaging almost a year later.

Preservatives are used in dog foods to protect the nutrients from oxidative or bacterial damage. The method of preservation of dog food depends on the form. Canned food is pressure cooked and sealed which aids in the preservation process. Semi-moist foods often have preservatives that aid in decreasing the pH and also contain humectants that bind water to prevent bacterial or fungal growth. Dry dog food has a low moisture content, and as long as the sealed bag is not damaged, environmental moisture cannot get in which deters the growth of most bacteria. The extrusion process of dry dog foods with high temperatures and pressures also help to kill existing bacteria in raw ingredients.

Best Used By Dates

Many premium dog food manufacturers have listed "best used by" dates on their packaging. Incredibly enough, no governmental agency requires dog food manufacturers to list this. Instead, many pet food companies use confusing code dates as to when the product was produced and where. Best used by dates are much easier to read and tell dog owners by which date the food should be used to ensure proper nutrient composition and decrease the risk of bacterial contamination and rancidity.

These dates give the average date by which the food should be used by when stored in average conditions. Dry foods should be stored in cool, dry storage sites when they are not being used. Most distribution storage sites and stores are air conditioned and will adequately keep the product good until the best used by date. However, storage units with high temperatures or moist environments may cause the food to begin to breakdown at a quicker rate. Thus, if your premium dog food has a best used by date, keep an eye on it, and be aware of environmental conditions that may accelerate your food's decomposition. If your food does not have a best used by date on its label, call the dog food company and learn how to read their code dates to find out when the produce was made and ask them how long it should be good for.

Of all the ingredients found in dog food, fat needs the most protection. Foods formulated for dogs contain plant oils, animal fat, and the fat-soluble vitamins A, D, E, and K. All of these nutrients have the potential to undergo oxidative destruction during storage. Oxygen attacks fatty acids and forms peroxides and hydroperoxides. Oxidation of fats in dog food causes a loss of caloric concentration, produces offensive odors, and can change the color and texture. Toxic forms of peroxides can be produced which are harmful to your dog's health.

Antioxidants

Antioxidants are substances which can block the oxidation of fats. There are two types of antioxidants: natural and synthetic. Examples of natural antioxidants are vitamin E (also known as tocopherols), vitamin C (also known as ascorbic acid), rosemary extract, and citric acid. A combination of these natural preservatives are recommended and probably safer than the use of just one. For example, most companies use tocopherols with ascorbic acid and rosemary extract.[1] Most natural antioxidants can be damaged during processing, so excess amounts are required to compensate for these losses. This increases the cost of the initial ingredients, and some private label or generic dog food companies either don't use them or don't include adequate amounts for long term storage.

Synthetic antioxidants include buylated hydroxyanisole (BHA), butylate hydroxytoluene (BHT), tertiary butylhydroquinine (TBHQ), and ethoxyquin. All four of these antioxidants have been approved by the Food and Drug Administration for various human and animal feed as a preservative in the United States. They also are relatively cheap compared to natural antioxidants. All four do well throughout the manufacturing process – that is they are not affected much by processing and cooking of the ingredients. Ethoxyquin has been used as an antioxidant in dog foods for over 15 years, and it has an especially high efficacy in the protection of fats. Because of this property, lower amounts of ethoxyquin is needed to do the same job as an antioxidant than BHA or BHT.

In the past decade, the use of synthetic antioxidants, especially ethoxyquin, has been questioned in terms of its safety. Two reasons surfaced causing concern. First, ethoxyquin has been used in the rubber industry to prevent oxidation of rubber. Secondly, it was listed as a potential insecticide or herbicide in the Merck Chemical Index (however, ethoxyquin was never promoted or sold as either in its history of use, and was later removed from the list in this book).

There have been many research studies on ethoxyquin in the recent years to determine if there are health hazards associated with its use. One particular study evaluated groups of two generations of male and female dogs fed 0, 180, and 360 parts per million (ppm) for 42 months (the FDA requests that the levels of ethoxyquin be less than 75 ppm for commercial dog foods). During this study, dogs in each group were mated and viable litters of puppies were produced with no long-term effects of the adults or the puppies. The health and fertility of the adult dogs, and the health and growth of the puppies did not support concern with use of this synthetic antioxidant in dog food.[2,3]

Most premium dog food companies today use natural antioxidants as preservatives because of concerns associated with the use of synthetic preservatives. However, to date, no research has demonstrated negative results when using them in recommended levels by the FDA.

JOCELYNN JACOBS

Considerations for Feeding Commercial Dog Foods

1. They are readily available.
2. They are easy to feed.
3. Premium and higher quality dog foods are cost effective.
4. They don't require preparation time.
5. They are regulated by governmental agencies to ensure nutritional standards are met.
6. They are regulated by governmental agencies to ensure ingredients are produced with safe and clean standards.
7. With premium and higher quality foods, ingredients are consistent from bag to bag.
8. In most premium dog foods, new research is implemented in ingredient choices which continually improves and enhances commercial dog foods, and formulations can be readily modified as new research data becomes available.
9. Some private label and generic dog foods (poorer quality, low-cost when compared to premium dog foods) may not have the digestibility or nutrient composition required for performance, pregnant, or lactating dogs.
10. Some poorer quality dog foods do not use adequate levels of natural preservatives to keep fat and other ingredients fresh for longer storage periods.
11. Some private label and generic dog food companies do not compensate for nutrient breakdown during the cooking and extrusion process. Most premium dog food companies adequately evaluate nutritional composition before and after processing to ensure enough of these nutrients are present in their initial product formulations.

HOMEMADE/NATURAL DIETS

In recent years, there has been much interest in switching dogs from commercially prepared diets to homemade preparations. The rationale for making this switch centers on a few concepts. First, dogs are carnivores, and wild dogs eat raw meat as a major part of their diet. Secondly, some owners have concerns about the manufacturing process of commercially prepared diets – that is, concern that during processing, essential nutrients may be destroyed. Earlier in this chapter there was a discussion how this can be true for some types of commercial dog foods (such as generic and some private label dog foods), however most premium quality food manufacturers typically ensure nutrient composition post-manufacturing and proper levels of quality animal proteins are used.

Nevertheless, it is important to discuss homemade diets since handlers of some performance dog owners, such as long distance mushers, use some form of raw supplementation. **The intent of this discussion is not how to formulate these diets, but rather discuss what they are and their advantages and disadvantages.** This provides "food for thought" for you in your decision of whether homemade diets are right for you and your performance dog.

Types of Raw Food Diets

There are three different types of homemade or raw food diets. First are *completely homemade raw food diets*. These diets are solely made from ingredients the owner puts together and prepares for their dog. The second are *commercially available complete raw diets*. These diets are sold by companies, and are typically in frozen form. And lastly, *combination diets* are those from mixing raw meat with either certain ingredients (cereals, grains, vegetables) or a commercial kibble diet (base product).

Completely Homemade Raw Food Diets

First let's look at those diets that are solely made up of raw ingredients mixed together by an owner (no commercial dog foods added). In recent years these diets have been unappetizingly referred to as BARF (Bones and Raw Food) diets. Some believe these diets are more advantageous because of the concern commercial dog foods might not have the proper levels of meat protein, fats, and nutrients to meet the needs of their specific dog. This may be true if one is comparing a poor quality or generic food to these raw food diets, but in general, premium foods have high levels of very highly digestible proteins, fats, and nutrients that the dog can readily absorb.

There are other owners that feed this type of diet because of concerns surrounding preservatives in commercial diets. With homemade diets, owners use "fresh" ingredients, and they don't believe there is a need for preservatives. Although these two advantages may exist, there are many more disadvantages.

The primary disadvantage to feeding a homemade diet is ensuring proper nutritional balance in every meal. It is extremely difficult to formulate a balanced homemade diet on a regular basis. Certain vitamins and minerals need to be kept in "check" with each other – too much of one can create improper intestinal absorption or increase excretion (loss through urine or stool) of another. In order to determine if a homemade diet is properly formulated, the diet must provide consistent levels of nutrients over a certain amount of time, and ideally should be periodically evaluated by a nutritional lab where nutrient levels are determined.

What about animals killed for meat and process by me, the owner? Are there more or fewer bacterial risks compared to slaughter-plant animals?

Animals killed for meat and processed (such as deer, rabbit, bear, and fish) by owners "may" have less of threat of bacterial contamination than meat obtained through some farm animal slaughter plants. This is primarily because there are fewer animals being processed at a time and in potentially cleaner conditions. Owners who game wild animals also have a tendency to clean and process them quickly after death of the animal and store them immediately in refrigerated compartments. However, cooking meat is the only way to ensure the threat of bacterial contamination is eliminated.

Another consideration when killing and processing animals for meat is having the ability to properly identify diseases within these animals. Sometimes animals are easier to kill because they are sick. At slaughter plants, trained veterinary personnel are on staff to properly identify contagious and diseases animals to eliminate them or their organs for consumption. Be sure to become familiar with commonly seen diseases with wild game to be sure you are not feeding contaminated meat to your dogs.

Dogs fed homemade preparations in the 1900's did not live as long as the dogs today. Improperly balanced diets fed over the life of the dog was one major reason for this. Nutritional research has consistently demonstrated nutrient deficiencies and over-supplementation causes certain diseases and conditions to occur in our dogs. If you opt to feed your dog a homemade raw food diet, be sure to contact your state veterinary or agricultural college to see if they will perform nutrient profiles on the homemade diet you are feeding.

The second major disadvantage of feeding completely homemade raw food diets deals with safety of the product. Those owners who feed raw bones or bone chunks may be putting their dog at risk for intestinal obstruction, gastrointestinal perforation (bones puncturing holes in the intestines), inflammation and irritation to the intestinal lining, and broken or missing teeth.

In addition, bacterial contamination is a serious problem. Anyone who has ever been in a slaughter plant knows that bacterial contamination is a real threat to the meat industry. Feces and dirty conditions surround the animals being slaughtered and during the meat rendering process. This not only puts the dogs that eat this uncooked meat at risk, but also their owners during its preparation. Cooking meat helps to reduce this risk, and should really be

---

Laboratory Evaluation of Homemade Diets

Very few completely homemade raw food diets are completely balanced for every nutrient. A study by Dr. Freeman and Dr. Michel clearly demonstrated this being a problem. Three homemade diets and two commercially prepared diets (one being a combination diet and the other a commercially available "complete" raw diet) were evaluated for various nutrients, vitamin and mineral levels. All three homemade diets had improper calcium to phosphorus ratios (which can cause growing bone diseases especially in large and giant breed dogs), various nutrient deficiencies, and excesses of other vitamins and minerals. Although the commercially prepared raw diets did better in their nutrient evaluations, both had sodium and phosphorus deficiencies, and excessive vitamin D.[4]

Of even a higher concern, one of the homemade diets had high levels of E. coli bacteria. Harmful species of E. coli can produce toxins that attack intestinal lining and cause clinical signs of food poisoning including diarrhea, vomiting, and potentially sepsis (severe, multiple organ infection and eventual failure).[4]

This study demonstrated how important it is to check that the completely homemade raw diet you are feeding to your dog has had proper nutrient testing at a university or nutritional laboratory to ensure proper nutrient levels.

considered for all those feeding this form of diet. Salmonella and E. coli are just two of the bacterial contaminate that could pose serious health threats to your dog.

Commercially Available "Complete" Raw Foods

Commercially available "complete" raw foods are those diets produced by pet food manufacturers intended to be complete and balanced without additional supplementation of vitamins, minerals, grains, or cereals. These foods are typically sold in frozen form and usually have shorter "best used by" dating than most commercially prepared dry or canned diets.

An advantage of these diets over completely homemade diets is that they are regulated by the same governmental agencies that supervise production of dry, canned, and semi-moist products. They are required to ensure their products fall within certain limits of nutrient guidelines. This makes them superior to completely homemade diets if a raw food diet is desired.

Bacterial contamination is still a major concern when feeding these diets. Because they must be kept frozen, delivery trucks and subsequent storage by the owner must ensure the product is kept frozen to prevent spoilage and additional contamination. The product still contains raw, uncooked meat from slaughter plants, and thus the potential for bacterial contamination during manufacturing and feeding still exists. This can still create a health threat to both dogs and humans. Handling of these products prior to and during feeding is critical.

JOCELYNN JACOBS

Combination Diets

There are two different diets that exist within this category. First are commercially prepared diets sold to mixed with various grains, cereals, and vegetables. They are not complete and balanced since they must be mixed with other nutrients to complete their nutrient profiles. This is a disadvantage compared to commercially available "complete" raw diets since it is impossible to ensure grains, cereals, and other nutrients needed to make it more complete are the same quality and digestibility from day to day.

The second type of combination diet is probably the most common among handlers of sled dogs. These owners use a premium quality dry food kibble and mix with it raw meat and fats. Keep in mind that by adding meat to these already balanced diets, some mineral balances will be disturbed. For the most part, adult dogs can compensate for some imbalances if fed them only over a limited amount of time. However, young, growing dogs may not. One example of this is with calcium and phosphorus and their delicate ratio. Meat is high in phosphorus. By adding meat to dry dog food diets, the absolute amount of phosphorus will be higher than it should be for the calcium:phosphorus ratio. This can have the most devastating effects on growing large and giant breeds of dogs, although the proper ratio in adults is critical as well for proper neurologic and other organ function.

In terms of potential bacterial contamination, the same disadvantage exists with combination diets as the commercially available "complete" raw diets when handling and feeding these diets. Thus, proper handling and storage of these foods is critical.

On the up-side, most long distance sled dog racers realize even the best performance dry dog food on the market can't provide enough calories these high powered athletes require to race all day long. By adding fat they increase the caloric density of the food without altering nutrient composition. By adding meat with some bone and cartilage, they can meet some of their dog's increased protein requirements without completely altering the calcium

KAKI ALMIRALL

to phosphorus ratio. Most of us don't own dogs that run over 100 miles per day for 10 days straight like Iditarod dogs – they are in a class of their own with special nutrient needs that can't be met solely with a dry dog food preparation.

Considerations for Homemade Raw Diets
1. Homemade diets are more time consuming to prepare.
2. If there are large numbers of dogs to be fed, it is difficult to obtain all the ingredients and prepare them on a regular basis.
3. Ingredient types may vary based on availability (non-fixed formula fed each time which can induce diarrhea or intestinal upset).
4. They are less cost effective (price per pound).
5. Unless a formulation is consistent from batch to batch and an evaluation of a batch has been done by a nutritional research laboratory (such as at a agricultural university nutrition laboratory), nutrient requirements may not be met in the dog for various vitamins and minerals in the proper ratios.
6. Bacterial overgrowth or rancidity may be a problem not only with the final product, but with raw ingredients prior to purchase.
7. May pose a human health risk not only to the preparer of the food, but also to those in contact with the feces of the dogs. Some bacteria is excreted in feces in virulent form and can contaminate playgrounds, dog yards, and show sites.
8. Owners may not be aware of new research presented to the canine nutritional or veterinary community to enhance their diets on a regular basis.

The decision to feed a homemade/natural raw diet should be carefully explored and investigated prior to feeding one to your dog. However, if feeding a raw diet is important to you, two types to consider are:
1. Commercially available "complete and balanced" raw diets that do not require supplementation of other nutrients, grains, cereals, etc.
2. A combination diet using a premium quality dry dog food kibble and supplementing with raw meat and fat or a commercially prepared raw diet that must be supplemented with a high quality kibble.

If you have decided that feeding a homemade/natural diet is right for you, be sure to read as much as you can before switching to this type of diet. A few books to consider are the listed in the References/Additional Reading section of this book.

APPLICATION TO PERFORMANCE DOGS

There are some situations that may require adding nutrients to a commercially prepared diet for performance dogs, such as adding fat to long distance sled dogs' diets. However, for most agility, obedience, and field trial situations, a premium quality commercial diet is more than adequate to meet their nutritional needs. Even most short distance sprint sled dogs and herding dogs do better being solely fed quality commercial performance diets than diets "tinkered" with by their owners.

When adding other nutrients such as raw meat, vitamins and minerals to a commercial dog food, keep in mind that delicate balances between ingredients may create more of a health problem than a benefit to your dog.

But if you decide feeding a homemade diet right for you, then be sure to read as much as you can from different and reliable sources about ingredients that provide a wide compliment of amino acids, digestible fats and proteins, high quality moderately fermentable fiber, and balanced vitamin and mineral compositions.

JOCELYNN JACOBS

References for this Chapter

[1]Papas AM: Antioxidants: Which ones are best for your pet food products?, *Pet Food Ind*, May/June 1991: 8-16.

[2]Monsanto Chemical Company: A five-year chronic toxicity study in dogs with santoquin: report to FDA, 1964.

[3]Monsanto Chemical Company: *Ethoxyquin Backgrounder*, December 1996.

[4]Freeman, L. and Michel, K. Evaluation of Raw Food Diets for Dogs. *JAVMA*, March 1, 2001. Vol. 218: 705-709.

Lonny's Show Career

   Lonny was a beautiful, AKC registered Irish Setter. He was a multiple grand-sweeps puppy winner, and after he out-grew the puppy class, his owner, Kim, decided to hold him back from the show ring until he was an adult. At two years of age, Kim began to take him to shows once again. He was in gorgeous coat - it shined and had the perfect texture. He had equally impressive conformation, so it wasn't surprising that he began to gather his points quickly from the classes. Lonny finished his championship in 2 months with 3 majors including a 5 point specialty win. He had all the other breeders talking and making plans of breeding to him.

   About a month into his adult show career, Kim was talking to another breeder who had just switched her dog to a homemade diet and was raving about it. Because Kim knew Lonny had the potential to be one of the top Irish Setters at some point, she decided changing his diet might be beneficial. Although he was a beautiful dog and seemed to be doing well on a premium dog food she had been feeding him since he was young, she was looking for that extra "edge." Kim wrote down the recipe her friend had recommended and began preparing a homemade diet for Lonny.

   Kim decided to wait until January (8 months after he finished his championship) to start his special's career - she was sure by then his coat would be even nicer and he would be even more competitive for group competition.

   However, when January approached, Kim was disappointed. Lonny's coat was not as shiny as it was before - it was course, brittle and broke off easily when brushed. His muscle tone was not as defined, although he still was on the same exercise program he had been on all his life. Instead of being shown as a special, he had to sit at home while Kim tried to figure out what she should do.

What was going on? Most likely Lonny was suffering from nutrient imbalances and deficiencies. One of the first places you will physically see differences with nutrient problems is the skin and hair coat. The coat is considered less of a priority for survival than proper functioning kidney, heart, or brain. Thus, the body diverts important nutrients to these critical organs, leaving the skin and hair coat to what may be left.

One thing Kim should have considered before switching Lonny to a completely homemade diet was reading as much as she could about them to gather information about which type of diets might work better than others. Also, she only did minor changes to the diet on a daily basis - alternating limited vegetable choices and not considering other types of animal protein which can be different in type of nutrients they provide. It was easier for her to keep feeding the same ingredients, but in the long run, it was hurting Lonny's chances of being a specials dog for the upcoming year.

Kim eventually switched Lonny back to the premium dog food she was using before, and within 6 months, Lonny's coat luster returned and he appeared more healthy. Although a properly formulated homemade diet might have worked fine for Lonny, Kim decided feeding a premium dog food was easier for her and Lonny did well on it.

JOCELYNN JACOBS

Page 3

CHAPTER 3

Dog Food Labels:
What They Do and Don't Tell You

What you will know after reading this chapter:

· What can and can not be determined by reading a dog food label

· What "label games" are and what they mean

· How can data from the pet food label can be calculated to more meaningful information

· How one label can be compared to another to determine which is a higher quality dog food

· What feeding trials are and if all pet food manufacturers do them

Whenever you go to a pet store, there are bound to be at least one or two people in the dog food section staring at the label on the back of a bag. Those people are hoping to decipher if one food is "better" for their dog than another. Unfortunately, there is very little obvious information on the label of a dog food bag that helps dog owners determine which foods are more digestible or higher quality. The reasons for this are two-fold. First, there are governmental agencies that allow only specific items to be listed on dog food labels. There is a minimum of information that must be provided and many things companies can't list on their labels. The result is dog food companies producing higher quality foods can not list things they might want to list such as their digestibility or quality of ingredients. The second reason it is hard to tell much about a food from its label is because some pet food companies play *label games* to confuse the customer into thinking their product is better quality than it really is. The only problem is, where our dogs' health is concerned, it's not really a game – it's serious.

REGULATION OF PET FOOD LABELS

All human and pet food labels are regulated by certain governmental agencies. These agencies regulate what can and cannot be used as ingredients and what can be listed on the label.

There are six different organizational groups that govern pet food manufacturing. These include:

Organization	What They Do
Association of American Feed Control Officials (AAFCO)	Sets standards for substantiation claims and provides an advisory committee for state legislation
National Research Council (NRC)	Collects and evaluates research and makes nutrient recommendations
Food and Drug Administration (FDA)	Specifies permitted ingredients and manufacturing procedures
United States Department of Agriculture (USDA)	Regulates pet food labels and research facilities
Pet Food Institute (PFI)	Trade organization representing pet food manufacturers
Canadian Veterinary Medical Association (CVMA)	Administers voluntary product certification

Of these agencies, the Association of American Feed Control Officials (AAFCO) is the most instrumental in setting standards for pet food labels. AAFCO ensures that pet food labels present information in an organized manner. They also ensure that minimum or maximum levels of certain nutrients are included in every pet food.

The Food and Drug Administration (FDA) specifies which ingredients are permitted in dog foods such as meats, plant products, minerals, and vitamins. They also describe acceptable manufacturing procedures for processing pet foods. Lastly, they are the agency that determines the criteria a dog food manufacturer must meet to label a food acceptable for certain health conditions. For example, if a company believes their product prevents urinary stone production, they can not put that claim on their label unless the FDA allows it. Such a statement is considered a *drug* or *health claim*. Although it is widely understood that pharmaceuticals can prevent or cure diseases, there is some debate as to whether pet foods can make such claims.

The Pet Food Institute (PFI) is a lobbying organization that represents pet food manufacturers, and frequently has members of larger pet food companies on its committees. This organization was formed to present and promote pet food issues to governmental agencies. For example, if a pet food company has done some research on a nutritional supplement but the FDA doesn't know what positive effects it may have on dogs, the PFI may help to educate and make recommendations to have that ingredient allowed in pet foods. The PFI also can make recommendations to AAFCO about label statements.

The National Research Council (NRC) is an organization that collects and evaluates research done on canine nutrition. Based on research projects done all over the country at universities and independent research laboratories, it makes nutrient recommendations for dog foods including type and level of nutrients.

The United States Department of Agriculture (USDA) is the governmental agency that regulates pet food labels. They determine what information is acceptable and not acceptable to have listed on each label. They also are responsible for regulating research facilities to ensure the meet governmental standards of operation.

WHAT IS REQUIRED ON A PET FOOD LABEL

These are items that MUST be present on a dog food label:

1. Product name
2. Net weight of the food
3. Name and address of the pet food manufacturer
4. The words "dog food" (so people don't confuse it with human food)
5. A statement of nutritional adequacy – if the food is made for a certain purpose it must be listed (such as puppy or senior dog food)
6. A statement that indicates how the product was tested to determine its nutritional adequacy
7. Guaranteed analysis which MUST include the following as a minimum: crude protein, crude fat, crude fiber, and moisture
8. Ingredient list in descending order by weight (highest quantity first).

That's it! That is all a company is required and, in certain cases, allowed to include on their dog food label.

Of the items required to be on the bag of food, the first four are self-explanatory. The last four will be explained more in depth.

THE NUTRITIONAL ADEQUACY STATEMENT

Believe it or not, dog food manufacturers are not required by law to feed their foods to dogs before they manufacturer and sell them. Some companies do, but some don't. AAFCO requires that dog food manufacturers do one of the following to assure their product can be safely fed to dogs:

Option 1 – Perform AAFCO-sanctioned feeding trials

or

Option 2 – Formulate the food based on AAFCO nutrient profiles

Option 1: Performing AAFCO-Sanctioned Feeding Trials

When a pet food manufacturer performs AAFCO-sanctioned feeding trials, the food is actually fed to dogs. Foods can be tested in dogs for just one lifestage, such as the growth period, or it can be tested in dogs for all life stages (growth, maintenance, gestation, etc.).

Performing AAFCO-sanctioned feeding trials is the most reliable and thorough means to test dog food. It is also the most expensive, and many small pet food companies and companies that make generic or dog foods poorer in quality do not use this option.

Companies that do AAFCO-sanctioned feeding trials have nutritional adequacy statements that look like this on their bag:

"This food is guaranteed nutritionally complete and balanced for all stages of a dog's life. This food meets the nutritional requirements established by AAFCO feeding trials."

With a statement that includes "feeding trials," you can be assured that the food has been fed to dogs prior to marketing.

Option 2: Formulating Food Based on AAFCO Nutrient Profiles

When a pet food manufacturer formulates dog food based on AAFCO Nutrient Profiles, this means that the food is formulated based on charts and number requirements for various levels of protein, vitamins, and minerals. Companies using this option are not required to do feeding trials prior to marketing.

Companies that formulate their food based on AAFCO Nutrient Profiles have nutritional adequacy statements that read something like this:

"This food is formulated to meet the nutrient levels established by AAFCO's Canine Nutrition Expert Subcommittee's Nutrient Profiles of Dog Foods for all life stages."

Because this statement does not mention "feeding trials," the food has not been tested with feeding trials.

THE GUARANTEED ANALYSIS PANEL

The guaranteed analysis panel is one of two things that pet owners look at most frequently (the other being the ingredient list). The guaranteed analysis panel lists the percentages of crude protein, fat, fiber, and moisture. These items are listed as "minimums" or

How important are feeding trials?

Feeding trials are the best way to ensure a dog food will meet all your dog's nutritional needs. By performing feeding trials, the pet food manufacturer will also be able to determine things such as:

- How palatable (tasty) the food is (acceptability of the food)
- How digestible the food is
- What the quality and amount of stool production is (a reflection of both ingredient quality and digestibility)

"maximums." Crude protein and fats are listed in minimums (example: not less than 25%) and fiber and moisture are listed as maximums (example: not more than 6%). Just because a label says it has a crude protein level of not less than 25% does not mean that this product has exactly 25% protein. It can vary from bag to bag especially if the company does not have a fixed formulation. The protein may be 25% in one bag or 28% in another. Of course, if a company consistently packaged higher than necessary levels of protein (listed on the label) in their food, they would not make as much of a profit since protein is an expensive ingredient. They are more likely to get as close to the labeled percentage as they can.

The guaranteed analysis panel gives consumers a rough estimate of protein, fat, fiber, and moisture levels.

Example of a Guaranteed Analysis Panel

Crude Protein	Not less than 25%
Crude Fat	Not less than 15%
Crude Fiber	Not more than 6%
Crude Moisture	Not more than 8%

All these percentages are based on an "as fed" basis as opposed to a "dry matter" basis. Putting the percentage in a dry matter basis takes moisture out of the picture. Dog foods (dry, canned, and semi-moist) all have moisture in them, and labeling on as "as fed" basis takes this more accurately into account. However, when comparing dry dog foods to canned, it can be confusing. Most dry dog foods contain around 8% (6%-10% is the general range) water. Canned food, on the other hand can contain 75-85% water. The guaranteed analysis for a dry and a canned food may look like the following:

Comparisons of Guaranteed Analysis Panels of Dry Verses Canned Dog Food
(Nutrient Content on <u>as fed</u> basis taken off a label)

Dry food X	Canned Food Y
Crude protein not less than 26%	Crude protein not less than 9%
Crude fat not less than 10%	Crude fat not less than 3%
Crude fiber not more than 4%	Crude fiber not more than 1%
Moisture not more than 7%	Moisture not more than 75%

Because dog food labels always report their nutrient levels on an "as fed" basis, to compare a dry and a canned food you need to compare the amounts of nutrients on a dry matter basis to even the playing field. When comparing these two foods on as "as fed" basis, it looks as if the dry food has more protein and fat than the canned food. However when both foods are compared on a dry matter basis instead of an "as fed" basis, it is apparent that the canned food has a higher level of protein.

Equal Comparisons of Dry and Canned Foods
(Nutrient content on a <u>dry matter</u> basis)

Dry food X		Canned Food Y	
Crude protein	28%	Crude protein	36%
Crude fat	12%	Crude fat	12%
Crude fiber	5 %	Crude fiber	4%
Moisture	0%	Moisture	0%

An easy rule of thumb to estimate the percent of a given nutrient in canned food on a dry matter basis is to multiple the percentage of the nutrient by four. Thus crude protein in Canned Food Y has approximately 36% (4 x 9% = 36%) protein. Once this is done, it appears that the canned product has more protein than the dry product. This would be true if the same amounts of each foods were eaten *with all the water removed*. However, because canned food also contains 75% water, the dog has to eat much more canned food than dry food to consume the same number of calories coming from fat, protein, and carbohydrates. Nutrients in canned food are diluted with water.

What does the guaranteed analysis NOT tell us?
1. It does not tell us anything about the amount of carbohydrates present in the food.
2. It does not tell us the type of protein or fat present (whether they are from animal or plant products).
3. It does not tell us about the quality of protein, fat, carbohydrates, or other ingredients.
4. It does not tell us about the digestibility of protein, fats, carbohydrates, or other ingredients.

It appears that the guaranteed analysis doesn't provide much detailed information about the dog food in question. Combined with additional information from the label, however, it can give you a basic idea of the nutritional value of the food inside.

JOCELYNN JACOBS

THE INGREDIENT LIST

After the guaranteed analysis, the ingredient list is the second most informative part of a dog food label. There are a few things to keep in mind when reading the ingredient list:

1. The ingredients are arranged in *decreasing* order based on the weight of each ingredient used in the food (so the most abundant ingredient is listed first, and so on).
2. The terms used to describe each ingredient are dictated by AAFCO.
3. AAFCO will not permit any single ingredient to be given extra emphasis (i.e., high lighting certain ingredients or making them in bold type).
4. AAFCO does not allow companies to describe the *quality* of an ingredient (i.e. Grade A chicken).

Because of these regulations, we face a number of obstacles when evaluating a dog food based on its label. First, these regulations don't allow companies to list quality of their ingredients. The ingredient panels of two different products may appear identical. However, the quality of ingredients in one might be vastly superior to the other. Manufacturers that use higher quality ingredients can not state the quality of digestibility of their product on their labels.

A second problem with these regulations is that they provide incredible room for marketing tricks or label games so that companies with poorer quality products trick the consumer into thinking their product is better or as good as certain premium dog foods.

LABELING GAMES COMPANIES PLAY

There are many different marketing tricks that dog food manufacturers use to mislead the consumer into thinking that their lower priced dog food is the same as a premium dog food. First, bear in mind that when it comes to dog food, you really do "get what you pay for." In general, dog foods that cost more have higher quality ingredients and higher digestibility.

The Split Ingredient Trick

Most companies know that we want to see a meat protein source, such as chicken or lamb, listed first on the label. However, many lower quality products don't have enough meat in their product to list the meat source first. So to make meat protein sources higher on their ingredient list, they take plant and carbohydrate sources and split them up. So if corn (for example) is their most abundant ingredient, it doesn't appear that way on the label.

For example, let's say Pete's Doggie Dinner's most abundant ingredient by weight is wheat. If they don't want wheat listed as the first ingredient on their ingredient list, they can split the wheat up into ground wheat, wheat flour, wheat bran, or wheat middlings. Then chicken by-products (their second largest ingredient by weight) – their only animal protein source – immediately becomes the number one ingredient because wheat was broken down into its parts instead of its whole. By doing this, we are tricked into thinking that their food is primarily made of chicken by-products since it is listed first on the ingredient panel.

> **Important!**
> When reading the ingredient panel, be sure to determine whether the primary source of protein is from animal meat or from plant sources. Animal sources of protein are of much higher quality and provide a wider array of amino acids, which is important to carnivores like dogs than plant proteins do (see Chapter 6).

Pete's Doggie Dinner
(ingredient list based on the most abundant ingredient by weight)
Ingredients: wheat, chicken by-product meal, meat and bone meal, corn gluten, animal fat (preserved with BHA), vitamin A....

However, when the manufacturer breaks wheat into its various components (playing the split ingredient trick), the ingredient panel becomes this:

Pete's Doggie Dinner
(using the split ingredient trick)
Ingredients: Chicken by-product meal, ground wheat, wheat flour, meat and bone meal, wheat bran, corn gluten, wheat middlings, animal fat (preserved with BHA), vitamin A....

Now chicken appears first on the list, but when you add up all the wheat components (ground wheat, wheat flour, wheat bran, and wheat middlings), wheat really should be the first ingredient!

Unless you knew about the split ingredient trick and you saw two different foods with these ingredient lists, you might think that the second food is superior, when it actually is the same! So, if you see a split carbohydrate source close to the top of an ingredient list, chances are that is probably the most abundant ingredient by weight in that food.

Sometimes a protein or fat source may be split on the ingredient list, but unlike carbohydrates, its separation isn't a marketing tactic. It may be that the manufacturer wants to emphasize the quality of their food's protein sources. For example, the ingredient list for Maximum Meal Time Dog Food emphasizes the fact that chicken muscle meat is used as well as chicken by-products. This dog food has quite a bit of meat in it, and its primary source of protein comes from animal sources, not plant.

Maximum Meal Time Dog Food
Ingredients: Chicken, chicken by-product meal, corn meal, ground grain sorghum, fish meal, chicken fat (preserved with mixed tocopherols), natural chicken flavor, dried egg product, brewers dried yeast....

The Quality Trick

As mentioned, AAFCO does not allow dog manufacturers to list the quality of their ingredients on their labels. Manufacturers of lower quality dog foods take advantage of this restriction and use poor quality ingredients in their product making it appear they have the same animal ingredients as premium quality dog foods.

A common example of how this trick is used is with the product "chicken by-product meal." There are many different parts of a chicken that can be used in dog food. A wild wolf may eat the entire chicken since it all is edible. However, different parts of a chicken vary in their digestibility. For the sake of simplicity, chicken can be divided into three quality categories:

- **High quality protein**: skeletal muscle (what people usually eat), heart (excellent digestibility)
- **High to moderate quality protein**: liver, kidneys, intestines, brain, eyes, stomach, spleen, reproductive organs (excellent to good digestibility)
- **Poor quality protein**: feet, beaks, bones, feathers (poorer digestibility)

The term "chicken by-product meal" can be used to describe any part of the chicken. However, most of the time the term "chicken by-product meal" is use to describe the second and third category listed (the high to moderate quality and the poor quality proteins). Unfortunately, regulatory agencies do not allow companies to state that their food uses higher quality chicken by-product meal (i.e. Grade A chicken by-product meal). Therefore poor and premium quality dog foods both may have the term "chicken by-product meal" listed on their ingredient label, but the quality and digestibility may not be the same. Feeding the dog food long term will help you determine the quality of chicken by-product meal – that is if your dog has a great coat, good muscle tone, and good endurance, the protein quality is probably good. If you don't have the luxury of waiting months to see how your dog does on a food, then use the rule "you get what you pay for." Higher quality chicken by-product meal as a raw ingredient costs the manufacturer more than poorer quality "leftovers" of chicken manufacturing (and that cost is passed on to you, the purchaser of the dog food).

The Variable Formulation Trick

Governing agencies do not require ingredients stay exactly the same or in the exact same ratios from bag to bag in dog food. So many food manufacturers of poorer quality dog foods use this to their advantage. This is called the ***variable formulation trick***. When a dog food manufacturer plays the variable formulation trick, the food may vary from batch to batch depending on what is cheaper that month or what is more readily available. Generic and many grocery store brands of dog foods have variable formulations. That is how they can keep their prices so low (some cost as little as $6.99 for a 40 lb bag).

Most high quality premium foods use a ***fixed formula*** – from bag to bag the ingredients are exactly the same in the same ratios. These products are going to be more expensive to produce since the company may pay more for the ingredients in the long run to keep them consistent.

How do you know if a company's food has a fixed or variable formulation? Generally there are three ways. First you can call the customer service number and ask them if they have a fixed or variable formulation. Secondly, look at the price. Higher priced products and premium dog foods generally use fixed formulas. And lastly, check the ingredient panel on several bags of a food over a period of months to a year. If a company continually changes its protein and carbohydrate sources over short periods of time, it probably means that the food has a variable formulation. Unfortunately dog food manufacturers are not required to change ingredient lists immediately with every batch of food.

Regulations only require that ingredient changes be reflected on the label within a six month period. Thus, if the formulation changes every other month but not radically, the manufacturer isn't required to change the label at all. This is a difficult trick for the average consumer to detect. Calling the company is a more direct way to find out this information.

Flavor Enhancer Tricks

Everyone wants their dogs to enjoy eating the food they buy them. However, many poor to moderate quality products use inferior ingredients and these might not be as palatable (flavorful). Dog foods with poor quality protein or little animal fat is not as palatable and dogs won't eat it. So, another trick companies do is adding flavor enhancers to their products to improve the palatability of the food. Market research has shown that people are more likely to buy a food that their dog clearly enjoys.

Garlic, onion powder, and garlic powder are examples of flavor enhancers used in dog foods. If the ingredient panel has these listed, you should ask yourself why. It may mean that the product is not very palatable on its own, either because of poor quality protein or fat sources.

> **What are some advantages of premium dog foods?**
>
> Higher quality or premium dog foods have the following characteristics:
> 1. Better ingredient quality
> 2. Better digestibility
> 3. Fixed formulation
> 4. Fewer, if any, label tricks
> 5. No flavor enhancers because product has high quality fats and protein, which naturally provide for good palatability.

APPLICATION TO PERFORMANCE DOGS

Performance dogs require a high quality dog food made by a company that uses high quality ingredients with high digestibility. They need to have a fixed formulation food so they don't have to battle with diarrhea from bag to bag because of ingredient changes. Choosing a good, premium dog food is half the battle in feeding a performance dog. The second part is feeding them correct levels of fat, protein, and carbohydrates to meet their energy needs and their body's requirements for growth and maintenance.

When evaluating a pet food label, look for the following:
1. Meat is the primary protein source.
2. Feeding trials were done (food was actual fed to dogs prior to marketing the product).
3. Animal fat is the primary fat source.
4. Split-ingredient tricks are not present on the label.
5. The product has the appropriate amounts of protein, fat, and carbohydrate for working dogs based on the calculated dry matter basis (see Chapters 6, 7, and 8).

Joe and His Quest for the Perfect Food

Joe was an avid field trainer with his Golden Retriever. His buddy Carl told him about this new food, Captain Kibbles, because it has done wonders for his dog. Carl told him it could only be found at a feed mill up on Blue Mound Road, and it was a brand new food that the feed mill owner said is perfect for field working dogs.

So, Joe went up to take a look at the food. Of course, the first thing he did was turn the bag over and look at the guaranteed analysis panel. It looked pretty good – 27% protein and 20% fat. It also was about $8.00 cheaper for a 40 lb bag, and that made it easier on his wallet. So, he took it home to try it out. After only a few days of feeding the food, he noticed his dog was producing more stool (about 4 times a day instead of only 1 or 2). About a month later, he started to notice his dog's coat wasn't as shiny as it use to be. Although she seemed to be working fine in the field, he was concerned about the amount of stool she was having and why her coat was looking so dull.

He decided to buy another bag of his old food so he could compare its label with this new food. The guaranteed analysis was basically the same between the two foods (27% protein and about 20% fat for both). However, the ingredient list was a little different:

His previous food's ingredient list:
Chicken by-product meal, ground corn, fish meal, chicken fat, dried beet pulp, brewers dried yeast....

Page 1

Captain Kibble's ingredient list:

Chicken by-product meal, ground corn, soybean meal, corn gluten meal, corn oil, brewers dried yeast, garlic salt....

Captain Kibble's manufacturer is playing the split ingredient trick. By splitting out the corn components (ground corn and corn gluten meal), chicken by-product meal gets to be first on the ingredient list. Also this food is probably not naturally as flavorful (it doesn't have any animal fat in it and little animal protein), so they added garlic to make it taste better.

Joe ended up switching back to his old food, and within a few days, his dog's stools improved and it wasn't long before her coat looked better.

JOCELYNN JACOBS

Page 2

KIM BOOTH

CHAPTER 4

Nutrient Evaluation:
How Good is the Food You are Feeding?

What you will know after reading this chapter:

· How nutrient evaluations are done by dog food manufacturers

· How to determine the digestibility of your dog's food

· How to compare two diets based on their digestibility

· The importance of a food's energy density to a performance dog

---

By now you know there is very little information provided by a dog food label – especially about important information such as nutrient evaluation, digestibility, and energy density. These are all very important concepts to consider when determining which food is best for your performance dog. How are these things determined, where can the information be obtained, and can any of it be calculated by information from a dog food label? All these are explored and discussed in this chapter.

NUTRIENT EVALUATION

There are two methods companies use to determine if their food meets nutrient requirements set by AAFCO's guidelines. The first method is doing laboratory analysis of the ingredients. Using this method, various tests are run to determine the moisture, protein, fat, fiber, ash (an estimate of the mineral content of dog food), and nitrogen free extract (a rough estimate of carbohydrates) in a food. This is a more expensive method proving their diet meets nutrient requirements.

A second method can also be used to determine nutrient levels: a company can take pre-recorded averages of nutrient content of the individual ingredients in the food, and then add the averages together. This method is cheaper to do, but it is not as accurate. Another disadvantage in using this method is that complete and accurate data of levels of specific nutrients of some ingredients may not be available. Quality of ingredients will also alter nutrient levels. Poorer quality chicken by-product won't provide the same nutrient composition as higher quality chicken by-product. Further, the act of processing (cooking during manufacturing) dog foods can alter the nutrient composition of the ingredients.

DETERMINING DIGESTIBILITY OF DOG FOODS

Because regulatory agencies won't allow pet food manufacturers to list how high or low the quality of their ingredients are on their labels, it is difficult to make direct comparisons between products. Knowing the digestibility of each food, which a direct indication of quality, would allow a better comparison between the two.

Regulatory agencies do not require a dog food manufacturer to evaluate the digestibility of their foods. However, many high quality, premium dog food manufacturers run digestibility studies to verify the quality of the ingredients they use. You can call the manufacturer to ask for digestibility results. If the company does not run digestibility studies or is hesitant to provide the data, there may be a reason. The company may not use high quality ingredients or is not proud of its digestibility results.

How are digestibility studies done?

The test diet is fed to dogs for 5 to 7 days during a pretest period to acclimate the dog to the food. Then the diet is fed for an additional 3 to 5 days, and the amount and consistency of fecal material is measured. The fecal material is then taken to a laboratory where the protein amount (or other nutrient is being evaluated) is determined. The difference between the amount of a nutrient in the food prior to ingestion minus the amount of a nutrient in the feces gives the percent digestibility.

Most companies use digestibility of protein as the gold standard to reflect the overall digestibility of their food. Of all the nutrients, protein gives the most accurate information about overall digestibility – if the food's protein is highly digestible, that usually parallels nutrient digestibility.

To determine digestibility, two methods can be used. The first is by chemical/analytical methods and the second is by feeding studies. Of these two methods, doing feeding studies is the best way to determine true digestibility of a dog food. The amount of a nutrient eaten minus the amount of that nutrient present in the feces provides a real-life determination of how digestible that nutrient is.

In general, there is an inverse relationship between a diet's digestibility and fecal volume: the higher the digestibility of a dog food, the lower the fecal volume. This is because the dog can digest and utilize more nutrients in a higher digestible food, thus there is less stool production. This is an easy at-home method to determine the digestibility of your dog's food. If the stool volume is low compared to the amount fed each day, the digestibility of the dog food is good. If the stool volume is high, then digestibility is lower.

Let's look at an example. Say Bowsen's Beefy Dinner and Fido's Formulation both have 26% crude protein listed on the guaranteed analysis panel. They also have similar ingredient panels. Are they similar diets with similar quality? To find out, we need to look at the digestibility of each diet.

	Bowsen's Beefy Dinner	**Fido's Formulation**
Protein guaranteed analysis (from back of bag)	26%	26%
Protein digestibility (obtained by calling the manufacturer)	73.2 %	84.6%
Fecal score*	4.7	3.9
Fecal volume (in grams)	154.3	48.40

*Fecal score defines the consistency of feces produced. A fecal score of 1 is watery diarrhea, while a fecal score of 5 is dry, hard stools (difficult to pass). In most fecal evaluations, scores of 3.5 to 4 are considered ideal.

Now multiply the protein from the guaranteed analysis to the protein digestibility, to get the level of digestibility for each food.

Bowsen's Beefy Dinner: 26% crude protein, with 73.2% digestibility
    26 x 0.7320 = 19.03 % digestible protein

Fido's Formulation: 26% crude protein, with 84.6% digestibility
    26 x 0.8460 = 21.99% digestible protein

Fido's Formulation is a higher quality diet because it has higher digestibility than Bowsen's Beefy Dinner. This is a good example of how dog food labels may have similar protein levels, but Fido's Formulation is a higher quality food because it has a higher digestibility.

Because it is more expensive to determine digestibility by feeding trials than by chemical analysis, fewer companies do them. However, it is much more accurate. Therefore, when you call a dog food manufacturer to ask for digestibility results, ask if these levels were determined based on feeding trials. Although the company may claim that either method is acceptable, there is just no comparison.

ENERGY DENSITY

When trying to determine which dog food is best for your performance dog, *energy density* should be considered. Energy density is the concentration of energy in a certain amount (cup, kilogram, pound, etc.) of dog food. Unfortunately, most dog food labels don't list energy density. In fact until recently AAFCO would not allow any reference of energy density on the label of dog food bags. Instead it is optional for a manufacturer to provide kilocalories in each cup on their bags. This is essential information to have for you to calculate how many kilocalories are coming from fats, proteins, and carbohydrates.

JOCELYNN JACOBS

The *metabolizable energy* (ME) is a term use to describe energy density – it reflects the amount of energy in a food available for your dog to use. *Digestible energy* (DE) measures the amount of energy absorbed across the intestinal wall. ME is more important than DE since it accounts for both digestible energy and energy lost through urine and released gases (burping or passing gas). Determining the ME can be done through either feeding trials (the best way) or by calculation (a less accurate way)[a]. So a dog food with a ME value of 454 kcal/kg means it provides 454 kilocalories in each kilogram of dog food. You can determine the ME of your dog's food by calling the manufacturer or doing a crude calculation based on the Guaranteed Analysis panel.

While calculating a rough estimate of ME, other calculations to determine the amount of energy supplied by protein, fats, and carbohydrates can also be done. In an upcoming chapter (Chapter 7), it mentions on average, 45% of calories should come from fat in a performance dog's food. How can you determine this based on the guaranteed analysis? First, convert the percent protein and percent fat from the guaranteed analysis on the label from an "as fed" basis to a "dry matter" basis. So:

% fat (from guaranteed analysis) ÷ 90[b] x 100 = % fat on dry matter basis

The same calculation can be done for percent protein and fiber from the guaranteed analysis.

This may seem confusing so let's look at an example:

Greenfield's Great Kibbles
Guaranteed Analysis

Crude protein	not less than 34%
Crude fat	not less than 22%
Crude fiber	not more than 5%
Moisture	not more than 10%
Ash[c]	not more than 8%

[a]ME is expressed as kilocalories per kilogram (Kcal/kg) of food. People frequently talk in terms of calories when discussing human food. In the dog world, kilocalories are more commonly referred to when discussing energy density of a product.

[b]90 is the amount of dry matter in dry dog food and multiplying by 100 puts the fat in a percentage.

[c]Ash may not be listed on every pet food label. Most pet foods contain between 5% and 8% ash. When doing calculations on dog foods, you can call the manufacturer's customer service number to get an accurate percentage, or use an average of 6.5% to get an estimate for other nutrients.

To convert crude amounts to a dry matter basis, take 100% – 10% (the amount of moisture in this product) and you get 90. Then divide the various percentages listed by 90 and multiply them by 100 to get the new dry matter percentage:

Nutrient	Back of bag %	Dry matter basis %
Protein	34%	38% (34 ÷ 90 x 100 = 38%)
Fat	22%	24% (22 ÷ 90 x 100 = 24%)
Fiber	5%	5.5% (5 ÷ 90 x 100 = 5.5%)
Ash	8%	8.9% (8 ÷ 90 x 100 = 8.9%)

Note the percentage of carbohydrates is not listed on the guaranteed analysis. To figure out how much carbohydrate is in a diet (based on a dry matter basis), another simple calculation is done. Take 100 minus the four percentages (for fat, protein, fiber, and ash on a dry matter basis) to get an estimated amount of carbohydrates in a food. In this example:

$$100 - 38 - 24 - 5.5 - 8.9 = 23.6\%$$

So, the amount of carbohydrate in Greenfield's Great Kibbles is 23.6%. To get a crude estimate of how many kilocalories there are per cup in Greenfield's Great Kibbles, another calculation is done using the percentages of protein, fat, and carbohydrates on a dry matter basis and multiplying them by an **Atwater Factor**. Atwater Factors are estimates of energy density. In dogs, fat provides more energy per unit (more than 2 times) compared to energy provided by protein or carbohydrates. Thus, the Atwater Factor for fat is 8.5, while the Atwater Factor for protein and carbohydrates is 3.5.

Nutrient	% dry matter basis		Atwater Factor*		Caloric density	Percent of total (kcal/100g dry matter)
Protein	38	x	3.5	=	133	133 ÷ 419.6 x 100 = 31.7%
Fat	24	x	8.5	=	204	204 ÷ 419.6 x 100 = 48.6%
Carbohydrate	23.6	x	3.5	=	82.6	82.6 ÷ 419.6 x 100 = 19.7%
Estimate of total kcal/100g dry matter			=		419.6	100%

(*Atwater Factors are constants used in these calculations. Note that fat is more nutrient dense. That is it has a greater ability to produce energy, thus its Atwater Factor (a constant) is higher.)

In this example, the ME (or energy density) is 4,196 kilocalories/kg of food. This calculation allows you to determine the energy density of the food you are feeding if the company will not provide you with it. It is only an estimate, however, not the exact amount.

APPLICATION TO PERFORMANCE DOGS

Determination of both nutrient evaluations and digestibility are important when deciding which dog food is best for your performance dog. Many companies will provide you with this information, but if they don't you may have to rely on how well your dog does on a food to determine its quality.

Energy density of a food is equally important, and it will help you determine how much food to feed your dog on a daily basis. Finicky eaters should be on diets higher in energy density – if they are only going to eat 1 cup per day, then make sure that cup is packed full of energy and nutrients they need. Dogs that will eat just about anything probably should be on diets lower in energy density or their daily consumption will need to be closely monitored.

> ### Kibble size can be important
> When considering energy density of a food, realized that a smaller kibble size may make the energy density of a dog food seem larger. For example, if you have two foods that are exactly the same in all aspects except for kibble size, the kcals per cup of the smaller kibble will be greater than the kcals per cup of the larger kibble. Some companies will make their kibble size smaller to increase the energy density of their food.

DENNIS GULAN

Stacy and Carla: The Poop Evaluators

Stacy and Carla both train top obedience dogs. Both have multiple OTCH titles, and have been training and teaching obedience for years.

One weekend they decided to go to a 3-day obedience trial together to save on hotel and gas money. They both had dogs that needed legs for their UD's, felt the judge line-up was good for them, and both liked the show site. Because they roomed together at the hotel, they would walk their dogs together in the morning and night. Stacy noticed that Carla's dog pooped much less frequently than her dog did. Stacy's dog, Kipper, would have bowel movements about 3 times per day that were soft in texture and quite volumous. Carla's dog, Max, would only pass stool once per day, and his nicely formed stools were small in volume. This made it much easier for Carla to pick up after her dog at the hotel.

Stacy asked Carla about the food she was feeding and if she liked it's performance. Stacy decided if that food helped Kipper have stools like Max, she was ready to make the switch that day! When she got home, Stacy compared Kipper's diet to that of Max's:

	Stacy's Dog's Diet	Carla's Dog's Diet
Guaranteed Analysis – Protein	27%	26%
Protein digestibility	74.5%	85.0%
Fecal Scores	formed but mushy	firm
Fecal volume	high	low

Although the percentage of protein is higher in Stacy's diet, its digestibility is much lower. This means more stool may be produced when feeding this diet because it is not as digestible. Carla's dog's diet is a little lower in protein, but it has higher digestibility which means less waste and lower stool production.

Stacy ended up switching Kipper to this new diet, and found her stools to be comparable to Max's stools. She also found that Kipper had a better coat (more shine and thicker), and appeared to have more energy for competition.

JOCELYNN JACOBS

JOCELYNN JACOBS

CHAPTER 5

Converting Energy to Motion

What you will know after reading this chapter:

· Which nutrients provide the most energy to dogs

· How performance dogs convert nutrients to energy

· Why different activities require different types of energy

· What lactic acid is and how you can prevent its build up in your performance dog

· How genetic selection effects energy utilization

Activity levels of dogs are just about as varied as the breeds themselves. Some dogs are low maintenance couch potatoes, some are active fly ball dogs, some are hard working herding dogs, and others are long distance sled dogs. So, it easy to see why it is such a challenge to appropriately feed your performance dog.

Energy comes from three sources: protein, fat and, carbohydrates. Of these, fat provides the most energy and has twice the caloric density of either protein or carbohydrates. Fat also is the only one that can be stored long term and in large amounts for future use. Carbohydrates can be stored by the body too but only in small quantities. Carbohydrates are stored in muscle tissue and primarily used for short, quick bursts of energy. There is no storage port for protein for energy use. Protein should primarily be used to build new muscle, repair injured tissue, and rejuvenate old organ cells – not used for energy. In most performance dogs, only a small amount of protein is actually used for energy.

For human athletes carbohydrates are a very important fuel source. Humans utilize glycogen (a form of stored carbohydrate) in muscle to meet most of their energy needs. Although dogs have a small amount of glycogen stored in muscle tissues, it is not their primary source of energy. Instead, dogs use free fatty acids derived from fat as their major source of energy. A pound of stored fat provides the dog with 3,500 kilocalories (kcals) of energy, while a pound of protein or carbohydrate provides only 1,500 kcals.[1]

ENERGY TO MOTION

In order for a performance dog to work, they need adequate energy. How dogs convert food to energy probably seems like a mystery. However, many research studies have been done to reveal exactly how this works.

Research confirms how important fat is for energy in dogs

Multiple research projects have proven the importance of fat for energy in dogs. In one research project, sled dogs fed high levels of carbohydrates and low levels of fat exhibited poor endurance and stiffer gaits while racing. In contrast, dogs on diets a high fat, low carbohydrate diet had better endurance and overall performance. They also had better limb motility and extention.[2]

Another study found field trial dogs fed a diet higher in fat promoted better endurance and overall performance than diets lower in fat and higher in carbohydrates.[3]

Although every dog activity requires energy, not all force the dog to use the same method of energy derivation. There are different ways dogs get energy from food depending on if they need energy for jumping, short bursts of loping, or running long distances. There are three primary ways dogs convert food to energy: *alactic anaerobiosis*, *lactic anaerobiosis*, and *aerobiosis*.

Three methods of energy production

1. Alactic anaerobiosis
2. Lactic anaerobiosis
3. Aerobiosis

JOCELYNN JACOBS

Different Sources of Energy for Muscle Work[4]

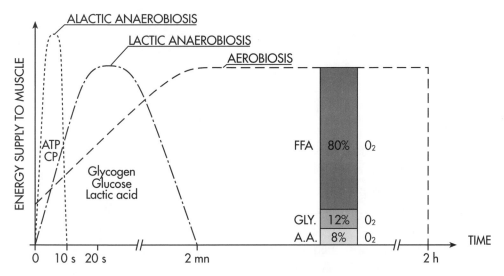

s = seconds   mn = minutes   h = hours   FFA = free fatty acids   GLY. = glycogen   A.A. = amino acids

METHODS OF ENERGY PRODUCTION

Alactic Anaerobiosis
A method of carbohydrate conversion to energy

The first mechanism of converting carbohydrates to energy is using the **phosphagen system**. This occurs in your dog's muscle cells. This system allows a small amount of energy to be produced in each muscle cell. This small amount of energy is only enough for a muscle to move for about 1 or 2 seconds. It is perfect way to get energy for a single jump or the first boost of energy to start a race. It also provides energy that allows your dog to jump and barking when the doorbell rings.

When fats and carbohydrates are broken down, what do they turn in to?

Fats are broken down into free fatty acids. Free fatty acids float through the bloodstream to other parts of the body (to organs, muscle cells, etc.) where they are used for producing energy. If there is an excess of fatty acids (more than is needed for energy that day), free fatty acids can be converted back to fat and stored in fat pads all over the body (ribs, hips, etc.).

Once eaten, carbohydrates go through various chemical alterations. One of the most important end-products is glucose which is converted to energy. Glucose can travel from one part of the body to another through the bloodstream just like free fatty acids. Organs and cells that need glucose will absorb it from the blood, and then converted it to energy.

Lactic Anaerobiosis

A second method of carbohydrate conversion to energy

The second mechanism of converting carbohydrates to energy is through the production and subsequent metabolism of glucose. After carbohydrates are converted to glucose in the body, two different methods exist to convert it to energy. The first method is called ***anaerobic glycogenolysis*** where glycogen (a form of carbohydrate and glucose) stored in the muscle is converted to energy. This is a common way dogs get energy 3 to 10 seconds after the beginning of exercise. The bad thing is that it only lasts about 30 seconds since most of the glycogen is used up quickly. There is only a small amount of glycogen stored in the canine muscle tissue, so it provides energy only for a short duration.

The second method is called ***glucose oxidation*** where glucose in the bloodstream and other tissues is converted into energy. For this to happen, glucose first must be absorbed by muscle cells. Certain hormones found in the body such as insulin, glucagon, growth hormone, and cortisol affect how much glucose enters the muscle cells. So these hormones directly affect how much energy is produced. In dogs, glucose oxidation is a good source of muscle energy but it only lasts 1 or 2 minutes. In humans, this is the method we use to derive most of our energy for exercise, but dogs are different and for them this energy source only lasts a few minutes.

In dogs, glucose oxidation provides energy at the start of a race, trial, or event when the dog is excited and first takes off. In long distance events, such as sled races or field trials, some dogs will use this energy in the beginning of an event or when they need a boost of energy to run up a hill.

I have heard there are supplements you can give dogs to stimulate glycogen rejuvenation. Do these work?

There are some supplements on the market that claim they support glycogen production during exercise in dogs. Some companies have good research supporting them. However, remember this type of energy is for short bursts, and it can't be used for long-term muscle energy. They may be beneficial during long distance racing or endurance activities (such as hunting or herding all day long) to supply the dog with extra energy to run up hills and jump over logs after they have been running hours on end. More research is needed to determine the specific benefits in using these supplements.

Aerobiosis:

A method of fat conversion to energy

The last and predominant way dogs convert food to energy is by oxidizing (breaking down) fats (lipids). Ingested fat or fat from fatty tissues stored in your dog's body travel through the blood stream as *free fatty acids (FFA's)*. FFA's enter muscles easily by diffusion. The process of diffusion doesn't require hormones or other factors to allow FFA's into muscle cells. The higher the level of FFA's in the blood, the more moves into the body's cells. Once free fatty acids are in the muscle cells, a substance called *carnitine* allows it to be transported into the mitochondria (an energy producing structure in cells) where it is converted into energy. The breakdown of FFA's is the primary source of energy for muscle for long term exercise. This is the way muscles get their energy from a few minutes into an event all the way through hours of prolonged exercise, as with sled, herding, or field dogs.

PROTEIN AND ENERGY PRODUCTION

Protein also can be converted to energy. To convert protein into energy, amino acids are converted to glucose in the liver which are then chemically oxidated into energy. However, it is important performance dogs do not depend

---

Primary Methods of Nutrient Conversion for Energy[4]
(relative intensities listed)

	Alactic Anaerobiosis	Lactic Aerobiosis	Aerobiosis
Jumping		+++	+
Race start	++	++	+
Greyhound racing	+	+++++	++
Lure Coursing	+	+++++	++
Agility		++++	++
Obedience		+++	+++
Field trial		++	+++
Water rescue		+	++++
Tracking			++++
Herding			+++
Hunting			++++
Sled dog racing			+++++

---

solely on deriving energy from protein because this prevents protein from being available to build muscle and repair tissues. Dogs with poor appetites are forced to use protein for energy because they are not eating adequate amounts of fat or carbohydrates. Thus, keeping working dogs fed on a regular basis to assure they have adequate nutrients for energy production is important.

LACTIC ACID PRODUCTION AND FATIGUE

Lactic acid is a by-product of the chemical conversion of lactic anaerobiosis, the second mechanism of converting carbohydrates to energy. Lactic acid production is normal during this type of energy conversion, however, excessive lactic acid production causes fatigue, poor endurance, and poor performance in dogs. Diets high in carbohydrates and low in fats produce excessive lactic acid in working dogs and can undermine their performance.

Excessive lactic acid production creates these problems for performance dogs:

1. Lactic acid production can produce hyperglycemia (excess blood glucose) which causes glucose oxidation to produce more lactic acid as a by-product. This creates a vicious cycle further damaging the endurance and performance of working dogs.

2. Excessive lactic acid production inhibits lipolysis, the production of energy through the breakdown of fats, making the dog unable to obtain adequate energy from other mechanisms. This will hamper their performance and promote poor endurance.

3. Excessive lactic acid production causes osmotic edema (water swelling) of the muscles creating stiff, inflexible gaits and poor limb motility.

Can the damage be undone if there is excessive lactic acid production? The answer is yes. At rest, lactic acid can be re-converted into muscle glycogen, but it takes vital energy to do this. Not a good use of energy for the performance dog, but it can be done.

There are some tips to consider in preventing excessive lactic acid production during exercise and training. First, feed your dog a diet with moderate to high levels of fat prior to the training and performance season. This will promote fatty acid oxidation as the primary source of energy

---

production and spare muscle glycogen breakdown during the off-season. Secondly, feed your dog a diet with moderate to high levels of fat during the competition season. And thirdly, keep your dog as calm as possible before an event begins. This will decrease the amount of lactic anaerobiosis that occurs and decrease the amount of lactic acid production. Keeping field trial, fly ball, agility, sledding, and herding dogs calm and controlled prior to an event helps prevent excessive lactic acid production. This is something that takes training and practice, since innately, these dogs are anxious to perform. Conserving energy for the event is key – it will ensure a better performance.

GENETICALLY ALTERING ENERGY PRODUCTION/UTILIZATION

Genetics play an important role in how efficiently a dog produces energy and converts it to muscle power. For example, the typical energy requirement for a greyhound is 150 - 190 kcal/kg body weight per day. A Siberian Husky, on the other hand, only requires about 100 - 110 kcal/kg body weight per day. Nature has genetically selected Huskies that conserve energy (by having a lower metabolic rate) because of extremely cold temperatures and poor availability of food usually found in Arctic-like conditions. Thus, the metabolic requirements are lower for the Husky than the Greyhound or most other dogs. Through the centuries, genetic adaptation to better conserve energy helps make certain breeds more efficient users of nutrients.

We, as dog breeders, also have genetically altered dogs improving energy conservation. By selecting dogs that are faster or better workers for our breeding programs, we are choosing better genes for conformation and structure. Also, when choosing dogs that eat less but perform the same or better than other dogs, we are selecting genes for more efficient metabolisms and better energy conservation.

APPLICATION TO PERFORMANCE DOGS

1. Assure your dog is being fed adequate amounts of fat and carbohydrates so they don't need to use protein for energy production.
2. Take steps to prevent lactic acid build-up in your working dog.
3. Choose the best possible breeding stock when producing the next generation of performance dogs. Chances are those dogs who are better performers with sound structure and conformation and those that require less energy to do their job will produce better performing offspring.

JOCELYNN JACOBS

References for this Chapter

[1]Arleigh Reynolds, "Figuring out Fats." *Mushing*, May/June 1993, pgs. 10-12.

[2]Arleigh Reynolds, "High fats vs high carbohydrate diets: How do they compare?" *Mushing*, May/June 1992, pgs. 22-25

[3]Davenport GM et al. Effect of diet on hunting performance of English Pointers. *Veterinary Therapeutics*, Vol 2, No. 1, 2001

[4]Taken from: D. Grandjean, Nutrition of Racing and Working Dogs. Royal Canin Research Centre, Saint-Nolff, Morbihan, France.

Do Hyper Dogs Finish First?

Bill had been sled racing with his team of 7 Alaskan Huskies for about 5 years. He would routinely finish in the top five positions. One summer, he purchased a few new dogs to put on his team from another sled racer. These new dogs were hyper and full of energy. They got his old dogs pretty fired up before going on training runs – something he thought would help his race times. Bill kept all the dogs on the same performance diet he had used for years and maintained a similar training program prior to the racing season.

The race season began and his team looked great in the starting shoot – jumping around, yanking on the harnesses, screaming to be freed from the people holding them back. He was pretty impressed with this new team and so were the spectators. Surely his new team would come in with the best time.

He did fairly well on the first half of the race, but noticed the dogs seemed to slow considerably on the second half. He came in with a good time, but not as well as he expected. The next day* his team was very hyper again in the starting shoot. After a mile or so, he noticed all his dogs seemed stiff and weren't extending their legs as far out in the rear as they usually do. What was happening to his "dream team?"

His problem probably stemmed from excessive lactic acid production. These new dogs were extremely hyper in the

*The second day of a sled dog race is called the 2nd heat – most sprint races are two day events with the 1st heat being the first day, and the 2nd, the second day – then both days times are combined for a final racing time.

Page 1

starting shoot – using up vital energy that should have been reserved for the race, and at the same time producing excessive lactic acid causing them to have stiffer gaits and poorer endurance. The previous year's three dogs were not use to all the excitement, and they too likely had higher levels of lactic acid production causing decreased limb mobility.

Bill had heard from other racers about excessive lactic acid production, and the next week during training, started working on keeping the dogs calmer when he was harnessing them up. Because he lived out in the woods with few neighbors or friends nearby, he didn't have anyone who could try to calm the dogs during harnessing and hooking up to the gangline. So instead of harnessing 1 dog at a time and putting them immediately on the gangline, he harnessed all the dogs first in his kennel yard, and then one by one add them to the line in front of his sled. That seemed to decrease the amount of time they had to jump, jerk, and scream on the gangline.

He also decided to play some tricks on them. He would harness up about 3 dogs, put them on the gangline, attach the sled to a tree, and then go up to the house for a cup of coffee! Or some days Bill would sit on a nearby stump and wait until they calmed down. Then he would un-harness the bunch and put them back in the dog yard. Needless to say, the dogs were completely confused. After a few days, they weren't as excited about being on the gangline because they thought they probably weren't going anywhere anyway! That is when he

Page 2

would talk to them, tell them how good they were, and then jump on the sled for a quick run. Over the next week, he only took them on training runs if they were quiet on the gangline. Eventually the new dogs learned not to be so hyper prior to a run, and his previous year's dogs became more mellow again.

During the races, it was a little harder to keep the dogs from getting excited, but over the next year or two, his dogs were much quieter than most teams in the starting shoot. Mr. Smith's times improved and he got a few more first place ribbons.

The moral of the story: Hyper dogs don't always finish first. They put on a great show for the spectators whether they are sled dogs, agility dogs, herding dogs, or fly ball dogs, but they waste critical energy prior to the start of an event.

JOCELYNN JACOBS

JOCELYNN JACOBS

CHAPTER 6

Protein Needs of the Performance Dog

What you will know after reading this chapter:

· What protein does

· What amino acids are

· How quality of protein is determined in dog foods

· What "nitrogen balance" means

· Why not all protein is created equal

· Which type of protein is better for performance dogs

When talking nutrition, most performance dog owners think first about protein. Protein is extremely important but not for energy production. Protein is more critical for building and repairing muscle and other organ tissue, and supplying amino acids for chemical and hormone body functions.

WHAT DOES PROTEIN DO?

Protein is found in every cell of your dog's body. It forms the major structural backbone of muscle, hair, skin, nails, ligaments, cartilage, and all the organs in the chest and abdomen. All body tissues are undergoing constant growth and remodeling, or if the dog is injured, repair. Without new protein provided each day, neither growth or repair can easily occur.

Protein is also important for normal blood functions. Red blood cells contain a protein called hemoglobin which carries oxygen to all of tissues and muscles of a working dog. Antibodies, which help fight infection, are also made of protein molecules. Protein is the major component of most hormones including reproductive hormones such as estrogen and testosterone, and hormones that regulate blood glucose levels such as insulin and glucagon. So protein is extremely important for working dogs – it moves oxygen and energy to muscles, regulates glucose levels, fights off infections, and helps repair old and damaged tissues.

Protein can also be converted into energy. However, performance dogs should not be forced to rely on protein as the sole energy source because of its important role in normal bodily functions and structure. Some human athletes use 5 to 15 percent protein ingested for energy during training and competitions. Although parallel research has not been done on performance dogs, dogs may use close to the same amount during an intensive workout.

WHAT IS PROTEIN?

Protein is made up of little building blocks called amino acids that are composed of carbon, hydrogen, oxygen, and nitrogen. There are 22 different amino acids that can be arranged in various ways (like boxcars making up a train), to make a particular protein. Different proteins have different amino acid compositions with different types of bonds (single, double, triple, etc.) holding them together.

When dogs eat, their digestive tract breaks protein into individual amino acids or groups of amino acids called **peptides**. Amino acids then are absorbed in the intestines and by the blood where they become available to make up other types of proteins for specific functions. When we talk about the daily protein requirement for a performance dog, we actually mean their amino acid requirement since they are the most important.

Because protein and amino acids cannot be stored like fat, dogs should eat protein on a daily basis to provide the building blocks for body functions and repairing injured tissue. If they don't eat protein on a daily basis they may break down muscle or tissues to provide the amino acids they need. Certain amino acids can be synthesized in the body. However, dogs can only synthesize

12 of the 22 different amino acids. The 12 amino acids they can synthesize are called ***non-essential amino acids***. Thus if your dog hasn't eaten a meal with protein recently, he can make some of the non-essential amino acids by breaking down other tissue or organ components. However, that takes extra energy and steals protein from other tissues which isn't always ideal.

The other 10 amino acids are called ***essential amino acids***, and your dog can not synthesize them. Ideally, all 10 essential amino acids must be eaten daily to prevent a protein deficiency.

NITROGEN BALANCE

Dogs have a daily requirement for certain amino acids and nitrogen, and both are supplied by daily ingestion of protein. A measurement of nitrogen intake and excretion by the body provides a rough estimate of the body's overall protein status, and this is called the ***nitrogen balance***.

Nitrogen balance = nitrogen intake - nitrogen excreted through urine & feces

A ***zero nitrogen balance*** exists when the intake of protein (nitrogen) equals the amount lost through feces and urine. However, some situations exist where a dog is in a positive or negative nitrogen balance.

Dogs with a ***positive nitrogen balance*** are eating more protein (nitrogen) than they are excreting: nitrogen intake > nitrogen excretion. Positive nitrogen balances occur, for example, in growing puppies and pregnant bitches when these dogs are fed well.

Dogs with a ***negative nitrogen balance*** are excreting more protein than they are ingesting: nitrogen intake < nitrogen excretion. No dog should have a negative nitrogen balance because the body is forced to use its own organ tissues to provide amino acids for routine body functions and growth of new tissues. Dogs that have a negative nitrogen balance are those who are underfed, are fed poor quality protein diets, have severe illness or injury (may not be eating or not enough to meet their protein requirements), and have renal failure or intestinal problems.

Performance dogs should never have a negative nitrogen balance. High quality proteins that are highly digestible (such as high quality animal protein) provide an adequate complement of amino acids in adequate amounts, and this is extremely critical in keeping a performance dog in top condition.

NOT ALL PROTEIN IS CREATED EQUAL

Every protein molecule is made up of different essential and non-essential amino acids. Therefore different proteins can vary tremendously in how valuable they are to your dog. Protein that contains abundant essential amino acids are of higher quality than proteins with lesser amounts of essential amino acids.

In general, protein from animal sources (chicken, beef, fish, lamb, or venison) is considered to be higher quality because it provides a more complete complement of essential and non-essential amino acids. Diets with protein primarily coming from plant sources such as corn, wheat, or soy do not provide as many different amino acids and may lack some essential amino acids. So if a dog food's ingredient label lists more plant ingredients than animal ingredients, it may be that it has more protein coming from plant than animal sources. Also, if the ingredient panel lists individual amino acids like lysine, tryptophan, or methionine (just a few examples), it may mean the company is having to add extra essential amino acids because the protein quality is not as good.

Now don't forget about digestibility – a protein has to be digestible and easily broken down into individual amino acids and peptides. If protein is poorly digestible, it means it can't be broken down by the intestinal tract which in turn means fewer amino acids absorbed by the intestines.

Let's look at some examples of different types of protein. Feathers and beaks of chickens are made up of protein that has a wide complement of essential and non-essential amino acids, but the dog's digestive system can't break them down into the amino acid building blocks, so they are of little value to the dog. The same is true of shoe leather. Shoe leather (from cow hides) contains a wide variety of amino acids, but it is hard for your dog's digestive system to extract them. So your dog can eat all the shoe leather he wants, but he will still be protein deficient.

Chicken by-product meal, a common ingredient found in many commercial dog foods, can range from being an excellent to a poor protein source.

Chicken by-product meal may contain large amounts of highly

digestible proteins from hearts, livers, and kidneys or it may contain poorly digestible proteins from feathers, beaks, feet, and heads. Because pet food regulatory agencies do not allow pet food manufacturers state the protein digestibility of their food, it makes it impossible to know the quality of chicken by-product meal in a food.

DETERMINING THE QUALITY AND DIGESTIBILITY OF PROTEIN

How can you determine the quality and digestibility of the protein in your dog's food? One way is to see how well your dog does on the food. Does he have a shiny and abundant coat, lots of stamina when training and competing, and appear healthy overall? This assessment can take many months since it can take months before a nutritional deficiency reveals itself in your dog's coat, stamina or general health. The second way to find out about digestibility is to call the pet food manufacturer and ask what the results of their digestibility tests were. The companies that do these tests usually are willing to share their information.

There are two ways pet food companies measure protein quality – by an analytical (laboratory) method or through feeding trials. Using the *analytical method*, there are three different analytical tests that can be performed: the Chemical Score, the Essential Amino Acid Index (EAAI), and the Total Essential Amino Acid Content (E/T). All of these

What are good protein sources for working dogs?

Because of the physical and mental demands on working dogs, their food should contain protein with a complete compliment of amino acids and be highly digestible. Look for ingredients such as egg, muscle tissue, and internal organs – generally these protein sources are higher quality and have a higher digestibility.

determine the quality of protein based on the types and levels of amino acids present. However, these tests don't provide any information about the digestibility of the product. Shoe leather or chicken feathers could score fairly well using the analytical method because they are only evaluating the types of amino acids, not whether your dog can actually digest and absorb them. Using the analytical method is easier and cheaper for pet food companies, but they usually are not as informative when it comes to feeding a real dog.

Doing *feeding trials* is a much more effective way to prove quality and digestibility of a dog food. There are three different methods that can be done using feeding trials: the Protein Efficiency Ratio (PER), the Biological Value (BV), and the Net Protein Utilization (NPU). Each of these three assays is performed differently – each with its own advantages and disadvantages. But here is the take home message:

1. Always call the pet food manufacturer to determine which method they use to determine protein quality and digestibility. If they use feeding trials, it will give you a better idea of the protein quality than if they use an analytical method.

2. Only compare different foods to each other based on the same method – whether it be analytical or by feeding trial. If two companies use feeding trials but one uses the Protein Efficiency Ratio (PER) method and another uses the Biological Value (BV) method, you really can't compare these two as accurately as if they were both using the PER method.

3. When feeding a homemade diet/raw meat diet not manufactured or packaged by a pet food company, determining protein quality and digestibility will be very difficult.

COMMON PROTEIN INGREDIENTS IN PET FOODS

What type of ingredients listed on a pet food label are examples of protein sources? A list of ingredients frequently used as protein sources is as follows:

Protein Sources Commonly Used in Pet Foods

Beef	Lamb
Brewer's dried yeast	Lamb meal
Chicken	Meat by-products
Chicken meal	Meat meal
Chicken liver meal	Meat and bone meal
Chicken by-product meal	Poultry by-product meal
Chicken by-products	Soybean meal
Corn gluten meal	Soy flour
Dried eggs	Soy grits
Fish	Wheat germ
Fish meal	

PROTEIN NEEDS OF THE PERFORMANCE DOG

Training and exercise will increase your dog's protein requirement. How much of an increase is still under debate. An agility dog probably has different protein requirements compared to a long distance sled dog compared to an average house dog.

No matter what kind of performance dog you have, however, dogs in training and competition have an increased need for protein. Training and exercising increases synthesis of plasma (blood) proteins. This increases blood volume that in turn allows the heart to circulate more blood to muscles with less effort. Training also increases the number of red blood cells allowing a higher supply of oxygen to muscles. Lastly, competitive dogs have higher numbers of contractile proteins in their muscles allowing muscles to contract better. They also generate a higher concentration of energy compared to untrained muscle.

Environmental temperature also will change your dog's daily protein requirement. In colder temperatures your dog grows more hair to keep their internal temperature constant, and hair has a very high protein content.

You also should keep your performance dog on a high quality protein diet even during the non-training/non-competition season. Some performance dog owners switch to poorer quality food during the off season to save money. However, if you feed a poor quality diet during the off-season, deficiencies may occur and that can cause set back in health and stamina during the next training season. If you think a performance diet is too rich during the off-season, just decrease the amount fed to your dog each day

I heard that high protein diets will hurt my dog's kidneys. Is that true?

There is an on-going controversy in the veterinary field about this topic and it has been going on for years. First, if your dog's kidneys are normal and healthy, then high levels of protein will not damage them. After all, dogs are carnivores that normally consume large amounts of meat. Where the controversy arises is when dealing with dogs with diseased, unhealthy kidneys.

Since the kidney excretes protein (nitrogen) normally on a daily basis, it was hypothesized that dogs with kidney failure should have lower protein diets to decrease the load and potential damage to their compromised kidneys. However, research done in the 1990's demonstrated that diets too low in protein were actually more damaging to the overall health of dogs (many created a negative nitrogen balance). Instead, moderate levels of protein have been determined to be better for dogs with kidney disease, so that the protein requirements for daily body functions are met.[2,3]

so they don't get overweight. If money is the concern, then at least switch to a high quality performance food two months prior to the training season to ensure strong, healthy tissues during competition. Remember – having high quality and highly digestible proteins available all year long will keep your dog in tip-top shape for training and competition season.

HOW MUCH PROTEIN DOES A WORKING DOG NEED?

Because protein can not be stored for future use, all tissue and blood proteins serve a purpose. If you feed a low level, poorly digestible protein diet, tissue and blood proteins must be converted to amino acids for other necessary functions. When these diets are fed over several weeks to months, your dog will develop a poor appetite, lethargy (sluggishness) and, over time, anemia (a low red blood cell count).

Because there are many variables in determining quality and digestibility of protein, no one <u>exact</u> percentage can be recommended for your performance dog. Further complicating matters is that dog food labels list protein levels on an "as fed" basis, not a dry matter basis – this makes it more difficult to compare one diet to another easily.

Most research on performance and working dogs recommends **30-35% of the calories in a dog's diet come from protein** (based on a "dry matter" basis, not an "as fed" basis in the guaranteed analysis of a dog food label).[1]

APPLICATION TO PERFORMANCE DOGS

Here are 4 things you should remember when determining which food to feed when considering protein:

1. Look at the ingredient panel. Is animal meat the primary source of protein, or are there more plant sources of protein listed than animal sources?

2. Call your pet food company to ask about their protein digestibility. Do they use animal feeding trials to determine the quality and digestibility of their protein? Is their food's digestibility high (80 to 90%)?

3. Do a calculation to determine if 30-35% of the calories in your dog's diet are from protein. This is what most literature currently recommends for performance dogs [Note: You have to convert the "as fed" percentage to a "dry matter" percentage (see Chapter 3).].

4. Most importantly, monitor your dog's health and energy level. When fed a new diet, if your dog becomes sluggish, unwilling to work, becomes ill, or doesn't heal quickly from injuries, he may be suffering from a protein deficiency.

JOCELYNN JACOBS

References for this Chapter

[1]A. Reynolds, "The Importance of Protein." *Mushing*, March/April 1993, pg 27-29.

[2]Finco DR, Crowell WA, Barsanti JA. Effects of three diets on dogs with induced chronic renal failure. *American Journal of Veterinary Research*, 1985, 46:646-652.

[3]Finco DR, Effects of dietary components on progression of renal failure. *Proceedings of the 10th Annual Veterinary Medical Forum (ACVIM)*, 1992, 460-462.

Roy and His Mysterious Sores

Roy was a 4 year old male pointer who was used regularly in the field for flushing birds. He was good at his job, and his owner depended on him greatly.

His owner noticed Roy was starting to get some sores around his carpi (wrist area), up his legs, and along the sides of his body. They were not itchy, but they would ooze blood and a clear liquid. His owner thought they must be abrasions from branches or sticks from running in the woods, and figured they would clear up on their own. But they didn't. In fact, they grew in size, and more sores developed.

His owner brought Ray to the veterinarian to see if the cause of the sores could be determined. Roy was very trim and solid muscle. It was easy to see he was a hard working dog. His owner said he would run about 10 miles a day in the woods.

Because skin scrapings of the sores didn't reveal anything, his diet was discussed. His owner had switched his food to a cheaper brand of dog food about 8 or 9 months before. Roy never had sores until a few months after his owner switched foods. His sores were normal trauma sores from running in the brush and woods, but it was obvious they weren't healing. The food he was feeding was mostly a grain based protein, and the digestibility was probably not the best. So the importance of a high quality, highly digestible dog food was discussed. Roy was put on a premium performance dog food, and sent home with some antibiotics for his skin. A recheck appointment was made for 4 weeks later.

Four weeks later, Roy's skin was healing very well. The sores were getting smaller with scabs now (no more oozing). His owner was running him in the woods the same amount as before, and no new sores had appeared.

A couple months later, Roy came in for his routine vaccines and heartworm test, and his skin was completely normal. He was still running in the woods daily, but no sores were found anywhere on his body. According to his owner, his stools were much better on this new food, and he seemed to have better endurance.

Roy most likely had a protein deficiency caused by a poor quality dog food. It may have looked like it had adequate amounts of protein in it (analytically), but if the protein isn't digestible, essential amino acids are not available to heal damaged tissue. His oozing sores were examples of how the body didn't have enough protein to repair injured skin. He probably also had a fatty acid deficiency causing an unhealthy skin and coat.

ELLEN GRABER

Page 2

CHAPTER 7

Fats:
Essential Energy for the Performance Dog

What you will know after reading this chapter:

· Common sources of fat

· High fat diets verses high carbohydrate diets – how they compare for performance dogs

· How to determine the number of calories your dog needs each day

· What fat requirements are for different types of working dogs

· Situations where too much fat is bad for performance dog

· What omega-3 fatty acids are and their benefits

Almost daily some article appears in newspapers or magazines talking about the hazards and health problems associated with high fat diets in humans. Because of all this bad press, people assume fats are just as harmful to their dogs. And it can be when it comes to feeding a couch potato dog – they can become obese and may have other health conditions because they are overweight. However, when it comes to working and performance dogs, not feeding enough fat may result in serious energy deficiencies! While humans utilize glycogen (a form of stored carbohydrate) in muscle to meet their energy needs, dogs use free fatty acids (a form of fat) in the blood stream as their major source of energy.

WHAT ARE FATS?

Fats are made up of carbon, oxygen, and hydrogen and are commonly referred to as *lipids*. Different types of lipids have different functions in the body. A group known as the triglycerides is one of the most important for dogs. Your dog primarily stores fat as triglycerides. They are stored under the skin, along muscle, and around internal organs.

Triglycerides are made up of a glyerol backbone with fatty acids attached. Fatty acids are an excellent source of energy for your dog's muscle and organ function.

Chemical Made Up of a Triglyercide

$$
\begin{array}{cc}
\text{H} & \text{O} \\
| & \| \\
\text{H} - \text{C} - \text{O} - \text{C} - \text{R*} \\
\\
| & \text{O} \\
& \| \\
\text{H} - \text{C} - \text{O} - \text{C} - \text{R} \\
\\
| & \text{O} \\
& \| \\
\text{H} - \text{C} - \text{O} - \text{C} - \text{R} \\
| & \underline{\qquad\qquad} \\
\text{H} & \text{fatty acids}
\end{array}
$$

*where R is different number of CH_2 molecules attached making up different types of triglycerides

Fatty acids are described by their length and number of carbon molecules. The position and number of double bonds that hold the carbon molecules together helps name and describe them. There are short-chained fatty acids, medium chained fatty acids, and long chained fatty acids.

WHY IS FAT IMPORTANT?

Fat is an important source of energy for dogs, but it also has many other metabolic and structural functions. For example, fat helps to insulate the body from extreme weather conditions and helps dogs maintain a constant internal body temperature. It also helps

LAURA REICH

to insulate nerve fibers, speeding nerve impulses in the brain, spinal cord, muscles, and other organs. Fat attached to protein, called *lipoproteins*, moves from the intestines to the bloodstream and then to tissues needing energy. Cholesterol (another type of fat) helps form bile salts which is released in the small intestines aiding in food digestion and absorption. Fat is also important as a precursor to certain chemicals such as the corticosteriods for normal body functions. Corticosteriods are released by the dog's adrenal glands in stressful situations, such as before a race or performance event. Fat also helps fat-soluble vitamins such as vitamins A, D, E, and K to be absorbed by the intestines.

Essential fatty acids are also a type of fat. Linoleic and arachidonic acids are two examples of essential fatty acids. Vegetable oils such as corn, soybean, and safflower oils as well as poultry and pork fat are good sources of linoleic acid. Arachidonic acid is only found in animal fats such as fish oils, and pork and poultry fat.

Essential fatty acids are important because they are the primary component of cell membranes – the lining covering cells in the body. Dogs with an essential fatty acid deficiency have dull, dry haircoats, hair loss, and eventually skin sores. With a long-term fatty acid deficiency, the skin can become itchy, greasy, and susceptible to bacterial infections because the integrity of the skin surface is damaged.

COMMON SOURCES OF FAT IN DOG FOOD

Common Ingredients that Provide Fat in Dog Foods

Animal Sources	Plant Sources
Animal fat	Corn oil
Chicken fat	Flax Seed oil
Poultry fat	Safflower oil
Lard	Soybean oil
Tallow	Sunflower oil
	Vegetable oil

In general, dogs find animal fat tastes better than plant fat. Dog foods that use more animal fat than plant fat generally are more palatable and provide adequate amounts of free fatty acids for energy use.

FAT AS AN ENERGY SOURCE

Of the three sources of energy (proteins, fats, and carbohydrates), fat provides the most kilocalories – 8.5 kcals of metabolizable energy (ME) per gram. Protein and carbohydrates only provide about 3.5 kcals of ME per gram. So, fat is about twice as calorically dense as protein and carbohydrates. The more fat a diet contains, the more energy dense the food and the more calories there are per cup.

Fats are broken down into free fatty acids in your dog's intestinal tract and then are absorbed by the bloodstream. Blood carries these fatty acids to tissues, organs, and muscles for energy. If there is a high concentration of fatty acids in the bloodstream and the tissues do not need the energy (their energy needs are met and the fatty acids are "extras"), they are converted to fat stored in fat pads for later use.

HIGH FAT DIETS VS HIGH CARBOHYDRATE DIETS

Over the years there has been much confusion about whether dogs perform better on high fat or high carbohydrate diets. The reason for this confusion stems from research done on human athletes. In the 1960's J. Bergstrom and his colleagues demonstrated that human endurance athletes on high carbohydrate diets had a two-fold increase in the muscle glycogen concentration (the body's form of stored carbohydrate). They also showed they were able to run for longer periods of time at a marathon pace. Thus the concept of *carbohydrate loading* was born, and it proved to be a successful strategy for human distance racers.

Because humans seemed to do better with high carbohydrate diets, owners of performance dogs began to wonder if this same concept would hold true for their dogs. However, in the 1970's,

What is the difference between anaerobic and aerobic exercise?

The difference between the two has to do with how energy is produced and used. Chapter 5 – Converting Energy to Motion – goes more in depth about the different types of exercise dogs do and they type of energy they require.

In very general terms, anaerobic exercise is short term, bursts of energy – especially used when strength is needed. Examples include running up a steep hill for 30 seconds, the first few minutes of swimming very fast, and jumping up and down at the beginning of a race. All other type of activity is aerobic exercise. Examples of aerobic exercise include doing a full agility run, running a race, herding sheep, running a field trial, and swimming long distances.

D. Kronfeld observed that sled dog teams on high carbohydrate diets exhibited poor endurance and stiff gaits while running. When these dogs were switched to a higher fat diet, their performance and gaits improved.[1]

So, why is there such a difference between humans and dogs? The answer is quite complex because of differences in cardiovascular physiology, locomotion, and energy metabolism. More simplistically, canines are carnivores – meat eaters. Humans, on the other hand, are omnivores which means they eat meat and plants in various combination to keep metabolism effective and maintain a nutritional balance. Although this may seem like a simple difference, when it comes to providing energy for working muscles and tissues, there is a large difference between the two species in metabolic pathways and utilization of nutrients.

In the 1990's a study was done to further investigate the difference between high fat verses high carbohydrate diets in canine athletes. Alaskan Huskies (long distance Husky dogs) were used in this study and split into two groups. The first group was on a low carbohydrate and high fat diet (15% carbohydrate, 25% protein, and 60% fat calculated on an energy basis). The second group was on a high carbohydrate and low fat diet (60% carbohydrate, 25% protein, and 15% fat on an energy basis).

The two groups were tested on treadmills. Both groups did aerobic exercise by running for 1 hour at 9 mph on a flat treadmill. They also did anaerobic exercise by running uphill (10 degrees slope) at 19 mph for 3 minutes. Blood samples were collected before and after each test. Muscle biopsies were also taken to measure the level of glycogen stored in the muscle tissues.[1]

The results indicated that during aerobic exercise, dogs on high fat diets had higher blood levels of free fatty acids available in their bloodstream for energy than did the dogs on the high carbohydrate diet. This was an important finding since high levels of free fatty acids in the bloodstream in dogs used more efficiently for energy for running or other intense exercise. They also discovered that dogs fed high fat diets stored more than

JOCELYNN JACOBS

twice as much glycogen in their muscles than dogs on high carbohydrate diets. This result was quite different than the studies of human athletes where they found high carbohydrate diets (not high fat diets) led to higher glycogen storage.[1]

The effects of high fat diets were still very evident even after two months of aerobic training. The dogs fed high fat diets continued to have higher pre- and post- exercise free fatty acid levels than dogs being fed high carbohydrate diets.[1]

The same phenomenon was further documented in Laborador Retrievers. A study demonstrated that Retrievers on high fat diets had an increase in maximum fat oxidation (maximum fat conversion to energy) compared to those diets with low fat levels. This particular study demonstrated that the amount of oxygen in the bloodstream also increased on higher fat diets.[2] What this means is that performance dogs kept on higher fat diets have more oxygen and energy available for hard working muscle cells to optimally perform.

DETERMINING DAILY ENERGY REQUIREMENTS

You now know how important fat is for energy, but how do you figure out exactly how many kilocalories (kcals) your performance dog needs on a daily basis?

It would be nice to have a quick and easy formula to calculate exactly how many kilocalories our canine athletes should be fed each day. Unfortunately, variations in size, weight, age, metabolism, and other environmental factors make exact calculations virtually impossible. Nonetheless, formulas have been designed to *estimate* your dog's daily energy needs.

These equations use your dog's body surface area, not their body weights. This is because the amount of energy used by the body is more closely related to body surface area. There is an inverse relationship between body weight and total body surface area. A large dog, like a Great Dane, has a smaller total body surface area per pound of body weight than a small dog like a Pomeranian.

Thus, energy requirement formulas refer to the ***metabolic body weight*** that helps account for differences in body surface area between dogs.

The general formula for energy requirements of an adult dog is as follows*:

Daily Energy Requirement (ME) = K x W $^{0.67}$

Where:

ME = the metabolizable energy

W = body weight of the dog in kilograms (kg)

K = a constant value that varies depending on the activity level of your dog:

K = 99 for a dog of average or routine activity: house dogs, some obedience dogs, lower level or early training performance dogs, working dogs with slower metabolisms – get fat easily, etc.

K = 132 for an active performance dog: herding, field trial, agility, some obedience dogs, greyhounds, fly ball, police dogs, working dogs with moderate metabolisms, etc.

K = 160 for a very active performance dog: short to some medium distance sled dogs, dogs with extremely high metabolism (have to eat a lot to keep weight on), dogs that hunt or herd all day long, etc. For some medium or long distance racing sled dogs, such as Iditarod race dogs, the K value probably needs to be even higher than 160. If your dog is losing body condition or weight then their actual needs may be higher than this equation recommends.

---

*Some equations use W $^{0.88}$ for large dogs while some use W $^{0.75}$ for small to medium dogs. Most commonly, W $^{0.67}$ is used as a general means in determining the average adult dog's ME requirements.

Let's consider two Border Collies: Zipp and Ping. Zipp is an active agility dog and weighs 35 lbs which is 15.9 kg (35 lbs divided by 2.2 kgs per lb = 15.9 kg). Because he is an actively competing agility dog, Zipp's K constant is 132. Ping is the exact same weight as Zipp (15.9 kg) but is a retired agility dog that daily takes 1 mile walks. Because Ping is an average dog with routine activity, her K constant is 99.

JOCELYNN JACOBS

Zipp's daily caloric intake should be:
$$ME = 132 \times 15.9^{0.67} = 842.4 \text{ kcal of ME/day}$$
Ping's daily caloric intake should be:
$$ME = 99 \times 15.9^{0.67} = 631.8 \text{ kcal of ME/day}$$

Even though Zipp and Ping are the exact same weight, Zipp should be eating about 1/3 more (on a caloric basis) than Ping. Zipp has a higher energy requirement because his activity level is higher (his K constant is higher which makes his ME value higher).

As another example, let's compare Luco and Blitz, both mid-distance sled racing dogs (same activity level). However, Luco and Blitz's weights are much different. Luco weighs 45 lbs (20.4 kg), and Blitz weighs 85 lbs (38.6 kg).

Luco needs to consume:
$$ME = 160 \times 20.4^{0.67} = 1{,}206.6 \text{ kcal of ME per day}$$
Blitz requires:
$$ME = 160 \times 38.6^{0.67} = 1{,}849.8 \text{ kcal of ME per day}$$

Because Blitz weighs almost twice as much as Luco, Blitz needs more energy per day. But notice he requires only 50% more energy (1849 verses 1206). That's because Blitz has proportionally less total body surface area than Luco.

Again, this formula only considers the total body surface and general activity level of the dogs. There may be other factors to consider, including:

1. **Each dog's individual metabolism** (how slowly or rapidly they burn calories). If Luco is a very excitable, hyperactive dog, he may need even more calories per day to maintain his weight than Blitz does.

2. **Environmental influences, such as temperature**. Perhaps Luco's coat is not as thick as Blitz's. If so, cold temperatures would increase Luco's caloric requirements each day.

3. **Fitness Level**. Perhaps Luco has not been trained as consistently, so his muscles may need more energy to do the same amount of work that Blitz's finely trained muscles do.

Equations to calculate energy requirements provides "estimates" and should be treated as such. A rule of thumb is this: Feed your dog the amount of food that maintains his weight. If your dog is more active than usual, the

temperature is cooler, or he has recently shed his coat, it may be necessary to feed him more. If it is warm, or he is less active than usual, it may be necessary to feed him less.

The above formula is for adult dogs with average energy needs. Puppies, pregnant or lactating bitches, and very hard working dogs may need more kilocalories per day.

JOCELYNN JACOBS

Caloric Requirements for Dogs with Special Needs

Puppies post weaning	2 x adult maintenance ME
Puppies at 40% adult body weight	1.6 x adult maintenance ME
Puppies at 80% adult body weight	1.2 x adult maintenance ME
Bitches in late gestation	1.25 to 1.5 x adult maintenance ME
Lactating bitches	3 x adult maintenance ME
Dogs with prolonged physical work	2 to 4 x adult maintenance ME
Decreased environmental temperature	1.2 to 1.8 x adult maintenance ME

CONVERTING ME INTO CUPS FED PER DAY

Now that you know the number of kcals of food Luco should consume per day, how many cups of food is this? To do this, use 2 more equations:

Equation #1:
Amount of food in kgs = ME ÷ Energy Density

Where:

ME = the metabolizable energy (as calculated energy requirement – Kcal of ME/kg)

Energy Density = energy density of the food being fed. Energy density is in kcal/kg. Your food's energy density may be listed on the dog food label. If not, you have two options – one is to call the company for this information or second, you can calculate a rough estimate using the calculations in the box below on this page.

Estimating the Energy Density
from the Guaranteed Analysis[3]

Step 1: Multiply the % protein (from Guaranteed Analysis) by 3.5 and write down the result.

Step 2: Multiply the % fat (from the Guaranteed Analysis) by 8.5 and write down the result.

Step 3: Add the %'s of protein and fat, fiber, moisture, and ash together and subtract the total from 100. This gives you the % carbohydrates in the diet.

Step 4: Multiply the % carbohydrates from Step 3 by 3.5 and write down the result.

Step 5: Add the result from Steps 1, 2, and 4 and multiply the total by 10.

Example: Step 1: Protein 28% x 3.5 = 98
　　　　　　　Step 2: Fat　　16% x 8.5 = 136
　　　　　　　Step 3: % protein + % fat + % fiber + % moisture + % ash = X
　　　　　　　　　　　28 + 16 + 3 + 10 + 5 = 62%
　　　　　　　　　　　100% – 62% = 38% which is the % carbohydrates
　　　　　　　Step 4: Carbohydrates　　38% x 3.5 = 133
　　　　　　　Step 5: Step 1 + Step 2 + Step 4 = Y
　　　　　　　　　　　98 + 136 + 133 = 367 x 10 = 3,670 kcal ME/kg (rough estimate)

Then use the following equation to convert amount in kilograms (kg) into cups:

Equation #2:

Cups of food = quantity of food (kg) x 2.2 lb/kg x 16 lbs/oz ÷ 3.5 oz/cup

We determined that Luco should be fed approximately 1,206.6 kcal ME per day. If the food he is being fed has 4000 kcal/kg, how many cups should he be fed?

1,206.6/ 4000 = 0.3kg x 2.2 lb/kg = 0.66 lb x 16 oz/lb = 10.62 oz ÷ 3.5 oz/cup = 3.03 cups per day.

Here is how these formulas work for a dog in an extreme sport – long distance sled racing. Research has shown that a typical 20 kg sled dog running the Iditarod can burn up to 10,000 kcals a day. The daily requirements for an active adult dog of this weight is 1,190 kcals per day. Prolonged physical work increases his requirement by a factor of 4, so 4 x 1,190 is 4,790 kcals per day. However, these high-powered dogs need 10,000 kcals per day – that is over 8 times the calculated amount just to maintain themselves on the Iditarod race trail!

If this dog is fed the same food as Luco, he would need to eat 25.14 cups per day! 10,000/4000 = 2.5kg x 2.2lb/kg = 5.5 lb x 16oz/lb = 88.0 oz ÷ 3.5 = 25.14 cups per day!

Can you imagine trying to feed one dog 25 cups of food per day?? The dog would be so bloated he wouldn't be able to run! So how does a long distance musher provide enough energy for his dog's daily requirement? The solution is to increase the caloric density of the food (squeeze more kcals into a cup) by using the power of fat!

THE POWER OF FAT

Fat is the most concentrated form of energy. By increasing the amount of fat in a diet, you increase the caloric density so fewer cups need to be fed. Iditarod mushers feed foods with a large portion of kilocalories coming from fat (versus protein or carbohydrates) to decrease the number of cups fed per day. That way these dogs can consume 10,000 kilocalories per day, but don't need to eat 25 cups to do it!

HOW MUCH FAT DOES A WORKING DOG NEED?

Because of the wide variation in types of performance and the different breeds of performance dogs, current recommendations are for dogs to receive **40-65% of their calories from fat**. That is not the "as fed" percentage on the dog food label – it is the percentage of calories coming from fat on a "dry matter basis."

A range of 40-65% may seem large for a recommendation. The reason for this large range is because of the wide variations in types of performance dogs, types of working situations, and daily requirements of individual dog's energy needs. Dogs that participate in endurance activities such as mid- and long-distance sled dogs may require up to 65% of their calories from fat. Herding and hunting dogs doing field work all day and short distance/sprint sled dogs may require 45-50% of the calories from fat. And agility, fly ball, sighthounds, police dogs, military dogs, field trial, and herding trial dogs may require 35-45% of their calories from fat.

Feeding High Fat Diets Prior to Training/Working Season

If you have sled or field working dogs, you may be tempted to feed your dog a more economical, lower quality dog food during the non-training, non-competition season. However, a better strategy is to begin feeding your dog a high quality food with slightly higher fat levels prior to the training season.

The level of free fatty acids in the bloodstream is a major determinant of how effectively dietary fat helps muscles contract. Dogs fed higher quality, higher fat diets prior to the training season moved free fatty acids from fat stores to the muscles to assist in contraction. These dogs became fit faster than dogs fed lower fat diets. This concept is called *priming the metabolic pump*, and it allows muscles to function more effectively when conditioning resumes.[1]

Recommendations for Amount of Fat as Dry Matter Basis

Type of Performance Dog	Recommendation Of Calories Coming From Fat
Sighthounds Military dogs Agility dogs Fly ball dogs Police dogs Field trial dogs Herding trial dogs	35 – 45%
Short distance/sprint sled dogs Day-long field herding dogs Day-long field hunting dogs	45 – 50%
Middle to long-distance sled dogs	50 – 65%

FAT TASTES GOOD!

Another benefit of fat is that it tastes good! Like humans, dogs love fat, and it enhances the flavor of food. Some performance dogs are finicky eaters during times of high stress or intense competition. Diets higher in fat stimulate their appetite and encourage them to eat enough to meet their minimum daily caloric requirements so they can perform their best.

TOO MUCH FAT?

Diarrhea

Too much dietary fat can be detrimental to a performance dog's health. Excess fat can overload the intestinal system and cause diarrhea in some dogs. Fat that is not absorbed causes water to be drawn into the intestinal tract from the body resulting in diarrhea. It's best to introduce higher fat foods gradually so that the intestinal system can acclimate.

Normal Stool

Diarrhea

Obesity

High fat diets can also cause obesity. Obesity can cause poor performance, lethargy, and mental dullness, and obese dogs are more predisposed to health problems such as metabolic diseases and musculoskeletal problems.

Bone and joint problems are more severe in obese dogs. This is a significant concern for dogs who compete in events that require jumping. In general, dogs that are in ideal weight and in proper condition can recover quickly from minor traumas. An obese dog that encounters the same traumatic situation can rupture cruciate ligaments, damage cartilage, or worse yet, break bones.

It is essential to keep your performance dog trim. Think about it – if you are in shape, you feel good and are physically fit to do just about anything strenuous. Dogs are the same – if they are in shape and in good condition, they will mentally feel good and be able to perform at their peak.

High Fat and Breed Particularities

Certain performance dogs require a higher percentage of fat in their diet. Many of the arctic breeds developed in areas of the world where their prey (such as arctic mammals and fish) contained high fat levels, adapt well to diets that are higher in fat. Other breeds, such as the Miniature Schnauzer and Miniature Poodle, tend to develop pancreatitis when fed high fat diets. German Shepherds may get diarrhea if fed high fat diets. Therefore, each dog's health and history should be considered when determining how much fat should be in its diet.

OMEGA-3 FATTY ACIDS

There has been much interest recently, especially in the performance dog arena, about fatty acid's called *omega-3 fatty acids*. They can be very beneficial to our dogs and thus deserve attention.

Where do omega-3 fatty acids come from?

Dogs can not make omega-3 fatty acids themselves – they must eat a diet that contains it. Omega-3 fatty acids are found in cold water marine fish oils and fats from marine mammals. It also can be extracted from plant sources such as flax and soy oils.

What do omega-3 fatty acids do?

Omega-3's have been found to be beneficial in fighting inflammation (swelling) in canine tissues. Inflammation of joints (arthritis); skin from wounds, allergies, or irritants; and intestinal lining are just three areas of the body that may benefit from omega-3 fatty acids.

How much should be in my dog's diet?

This is a tricky question. The absolute amount required by each dog may vary, and overdoses of omega-3's can be detrimental to your dog's health. A diet too high in omega-3 fatty acids can interfere with blood clotting and promote bleeding tendencies. However, studies done looked at how certain levels of omega-3 fatty acids could promote the positive effects of inflammation control, but avoid clotting problems. It was found the *ratio* between omega-6 fatty acids and omega-3 fatty acids is actually more important than the absolute amount of omega-3 fatty acids.

Omega-6 fatty acids, such as linoleic and arachidonic acids, are essential fatty acids, and must be eaten daily to maintain good health. Omega-6 fatty acids are important for healthy skin and other tissues, and deficiencies can be problematic.

Why is the ratio of omega-6 fatty acids to omega-3 fatty acids important? It turns out that omega-3 fatty acids and some omega-6 fatty acids are broken down by similar enzymatic pathways. Thus they compete for the same enzymes to produce their end products or metabolites. The metabolites of omega-3 fatty acids inhibit inflammation, whereas the metabolites of omega-6 fatty acids promote inflammation.

DENNIS GULAN

By ensuring a balance between these two types of omega fatty acids in your dog's diet, you can reduce the number of pro-inflammatory metabolites. An ideal ratio between these two types of fatty acids will help decrease inflammation. The ratio was determined to be between 5:1 to 10:1. In other words, for every 5 to 10 omega-6 fatty acids, 1 omega-3 fatty acid should be consumed.[4]

Providing the proper ratio of omega fatty acids to working dogs may help combat minor injuries and enhance the healing process. Many dog foods on the market today have the proper ratio of omega-6 fatty acids and omega-3 fatty acids which takes the guess work out of how much omega-3 fatty acids to add to achieve this balance. Some diets even list the levels and ratio of omega-6 and omega-3 fatty acids. Remember, diets too high in omega-3 fatty acids can cause blood clotting problems, so until research proves different, it is ideal to keep the ratio close to this range.

APPLICATION TO PERFORMANCE DOGS

Here are some things to consider when considering fat:

1. Determine the quality of fat in the diet by evaluating the dog food label. Is animal fat the primary source of fat?

2. Check that the appropriate amount of calories are coming from fat for your particular working dog situation. If you have an agility dog, the recommended levels of fat will be different than if you have a long distance sled dog. Note that you must convert the fat on the dog food label from an "as fed" percentage to a "dry matter" basis to see if you are feeding your dog the correct levels of fat.

3. Monitor your dog's body condition score on a regular basis (see Chapter 11) to be sure they are not being fed too many calories and too much fat. Overweight dogs will not perform at their best, and may be susceptible to serious bone, joint, or muscle injuries.

References for this Chapter

[1]Reynolds, A. High-Fat vs. High-Carbohydrate Diets: How Do They Compare? *Mushing*, May/June 1992, pgs 22-25.

[2]Reynolds, AJ and Reinhart GA. The Role of Fat in the Formulation of Performance Rations: Focus on Fat Sources. In *Recent Advances in Canine and Feline Nutrition Volume II*. Wilmington, OH: Orange Frazier Press, 1998; 277-282.

[3]D. Dzanis. Feeding Puppies and Kittens For Optimum Growth and Health. *DVM News Magazine Best Practices*, June 2002, pg 22.

[4]Vaughn, DM and Reinhart GA. Influence of Dietary Fatty Acid Ratios on Tissue Eicosanoid Production and Blood Coagulation Parameters in Dogs. In Reinhart, GA and Carey DP, eds. *Recent Advances in Canine and Feline Nutritional Research Volume I*. Wilmington, OH: Orange Frazier Press, 1996; 243-256.

Chuck and Maintaining His Weight

Chuck was 4 year old, high energy Jack Russell Terrier. His claim to fame was agility – he lived for running the course.

However, his owner had a hard time keeping weight on him. He was small so she didn't want to feed him too many cups at a time to make him bloat. Chuck also was a finicky eater – he would rather starve 3 days than take time out of his busy routine to eat. When they would go to many competitions in a row, Chuck's owner would see his weight drop quickly, and she was worried his nutrient and energy needs would not be met.

In Chuck's case, his owner needed to make sure the food he was being fed had the proper amount of calories coming from fat (35-45%, but with him being active, he really should be at the high end of the range – closer to 45%). This would allow him to get more energy per cup of food. Because he was a finicky eater, a diet higher in animal fat would help stimulate his appetite. Diets with animal protein (verses plant protein) also are more palatable and should be considered. Some dogs also like to have a little canned food mixed in with their dry food or water added. Lastly, by feeding multiple small meals per day (verses just one or two bigger ones), his nutrient and energy requirements might better be met.

In Chuck's case, his owner switched to a premium performance food that had 45% of its calories coming from fat (based on a dry matter basis). She also added a little puppy canned food to his dry food, and fed him three small meals per day verses one. This helped him eat better, and he

Page 1

began to keep his weight on. Over time, she was able to cut his meals to twice a day, and feed less canned food while still maintaining his weight.

JOCELYNN JACOBS

Page 2

KOHLER PHOTOGRAPHY

Carbohydrate Needs of the Performance Dog

What you will know after reading this chapter:

· Why carbohydrates are important in a working dog's diet

· Some common sources of carbohydrates

· How much of the performance dog's diet should be carbohydrates

· What fiber is and its importance

After reading the last chapter on fats, you may wonder why working dogs need carbohydrates in their diet at all. However, carbohydrates are important – they provide many nutrients not found in protein or fat, and without them, dogs have a tendency to get diarrhea.

WHAT ARE CARBOHYDRATES?

Carbohydrates are combinations of carbon, hydrogen, and oxygen, and primarily come from plant material. Carbohydrates can be classified in three categories:

1. monosaccharides ("mono" means one, so these are single sugars)
2. disaccharides ("di" means two, so these are double sugars linked together)
3. polysaccharides ("poly" means many, so these are multiple sugars linked together)

Monosaccharides are simple sugars such as glucose, fructose, and galactose. Glucose is a simple sugar found in fruits and berries, and in commercially prepared products such as corn syrup. Carbohydrates circulate in your dog's blood in the form of glucose which provides nutrients for muscles and organs.

Another simple sugar is fructose, and it is found in honey, ripe fruits, and vegetables.

Galactose is not found by itself, instead it makes up half of the disaccharide lactose which is present in the milk of mammals. Lactose is made up of a galactose molecule and a glucose molecule. In the intestines, lactose is broken down releasing galactose which then goes to the liver to be converted to glucose for tissue and muscle absorption.

Sucrose is another disaccharide. Sucrose is more commonly known as table sugar, and it is composed of fructose and glucose. It is naturally found in foods such as sugar cane, beets, and maple syrup.

Polysaccharides are made up of many simple sugars all linked together to form long chains. Starch, glycogen, dextrins, and dietary fiber are all examples of types of polysaccharides. Corn, wheat, and rice are all starches, the major source of carbohydrates in most pet foods. Glycogen is a stored form of carbohydrate found in your dog's muscle and liver.

Dietary fiber is also a type of polysaccharide. Cellulose, hemi-cellulose, pectin, and plant gums are all examples of dietary fiber. Fiber can not be digested by the dog's intestinal tract because it doesn't have the proper enzymes, but bacteria living in the intestines do. Most fibers are digested by intestinal bacteria, a process called *fermentation*.

WHAT DO CARBOHYDRATES DO?

Carbohydrates are broken down into glucose to be used for energy and other body functions. Although glucose is not the primary source of energy for dogs, it can be helpful in providing "boosts" of energy when jumping, running up hills, or during the beginning or end of a race. Carbohydrates are only half as energy dense as fats, providing only 3.5kcal ME/gram.

Glucose is also important for keeping the nervous system (brain and nerves) functioning well. Dogs with a low blood glucose level will become lethargic and may seizure if levels get too low.

Dietary carbohydrates also provide carbon molecules to produce other important things such as non-essential amino acids.

Carbohydrates in the form of fiber can be helpful in maintaining a healthy intestinal tract. Certain moderately fermentable fibers, such as rice bran and beet pulp, provide energy for cells of the intestinal lining promoting its health and well-being. Fiber effects stool quality. Fibers like cellulose cause hard dry stools while others like guar gum produce running, less formed stools.

COMMON SOURCES OF CARBOHYDRATES IN PET FOODS

Common sources of carbohydrates in dog foods

Alfalfa meal	Ground wheat
Barley	Molasses
Brewer's rice	Oats
Brown rice	Oat meal
Corn (ground)	Pearled barley
Dried kelp	Potatoes
Dried whey	Rice flour
Flax seed	Sorghum
Flax seed meal	Wheat
Corn (ground)	Wheat flour

HOW MUCH CARBOHYDRATE DOES A WORKING DOG NEED?

Most research on performance and working dogs recommends **10-15% of the calories come from carbohydrates** (based on a "dry matter" basis).

DIETARY FIBER AND INTESTINAL HEALTH

Until recent years, dietary fiber was categorized as soluble or insoluble fiber. However, recently many nutritional sources now categorizing fibers in terms of their fermentability – a more accurate and meaningful way to measure the usability of fiber to the intestinal tract. Fiber is digested by bacteria living in the intestinal tract into smaller, more usable components. Fermentability is defined as how easily a fiber is broken down by intestinal bacteria.

Relationship Between Solubility and Fermentability[1]

Fiber	Fermentability
Beet pulp	Moderate
Cellulose	Low
Rice bran	Moderate
Gum arabic	Moderate
Pectin	High
C-M cellulose	Low
Methylcellulose	Low
Cabbage fiber	High
Guar gum	High
Locust bean gum	Low
Xanthan gum	Moderate

Fiber is broken down to produce short-chained fatty acids (SCFA) and other by-products. The three most abundant SCFA's produced are acetate, propionate, and butyrate by the fermentation process. How many SCFA's are produced depends on the type of fiber, how long it is in the intestinal tract (short time with diarrhea or long time with constipation), and if there are other dietary components present that interfere with the fermentation process.

Dogs benefit tremendously from bacterial production of SCFA's. This is because cells lining the large intestine have a very high turnover rate and they depend on SCFA's as a significant source of energy. By feeding fiber that promotes abundant SCFA production, the lining of the intestine becomes healthier. This is important to reduce the incidence of diarrhea.[1,2]

DENNIS GULAN

COMMON SOURCES OF FIBER IN PET FOODS
Common ingredients that provide fiber in dog foods

Apple pomace	Pearled barley
Barley	Rice bran
Beet pulp	Soybean hulls
Cellulose	Soybean mill run
Citrus pulp	Tomato pomace
Oat bran	
Peanut hulls	

WHAT TYPES OF FIBER SHOULD BE INCLUDED IN A DIET?

Moderately fermentable fibers appear to be the most beneficial to dogs' intestinal tracts. Low fermentability fibers do not provide adequate levels of SCFA's, while high fermentability fibers produce excess gas and sometimes diarrhea. Beet pulp and rice bran are two fiber sources that appear to be the most effective in producing an adequate amount of SCFA's while maintaining good stool quality.[3]

HOW MUCH FIBER SHOULD THERE BE?

Most research recommends **fiber levels of 3-7%** (based on a "dry matter" basis) in dog food. For the most part, fiber listed on the guaranteed analysis of a dog food label is usually close to the "as fed" amount because of its low percentage.

APPLICATION TO PERFORMANCE DOGS

Although more emphasis is generally given to protein and fat, carbohydrates also are a very important part of your working dog's diet. Diets with too little carbohydrate can cause diarrhea potentially can cause deficiencies of important nutrients.

Fiber is not just for cows and horses either! In dogs, moderately fermentable fibers, such as beet pulp and rice bran, can promote a healthy intestinal lining.

JOCELYNN JACOBS

References for this Chapter

[1]The Iams Company, Topics in Practical Nutrition – Advances in Fiber Nutrition, Volume 4, number 2, June 1994.

[2]Kerley, M, and Sunvold, G. Physiological Response to Short Chain Fatty Acid Production in the Intestine. In Reinhart, GA and Carey DP, eds. *Recent Advances in Canine and Feline Nutrition Volume I.* Wilmington, OH: Orange Frazier Press, 1996; 33-39.

[3]Clemens ET. Dietary Fiber and Colonic Morphology. In Reinhart, GA and Carey DP, eds. *Recent Advances in Canine and Feline Nutrition Volume I.* Wilmington, OH: Orange Frazier Press, 1996; 25-32.

Keeper and Chronic Diarrhea

Keeper was a 7 year old Golden Retriever who had mild diarrhea (cow-pie consistency stools) for over 3 months. Her owners had her stool sample checked by their veterinarian and she was wormed with a broad spectum wormer even though her stools did not show any signs of worms. Although she had a healthy appetite, she began to lose weight. Her performance at fly ball competitions began to falter, and some people on her team were concerned Keeper wasn't acting her normal perky self.

Keeper's bloodwork and urine samples were completely normal. Xrays of her abdomen also appeared normal. Her veterinarian decided to do a biopsy of her intestines to see if she had an irritated bowel lining causing poor absorption and chronic diarrhea.

Her biopsy came back positive for inflammatory bowel disease (IBD) causing the lining of her intestines to be irritated and fill with inflammatory cells. Treatment consisted of antibiotics and cortisone and a change in diet to help improve the health of her intestines. The diet chosen was a veterinary prescription diet called Eukanuba Veterinary Diet Low Residue for Dogs™, and in it were proper levels of fatty acids to decrease inflammation of her bowel lining, highly digestible nutrients for high absorption, beet pulp to promote a healthier intestinal lining, and fructooligiosaccharides to maintain healthy bacterial counts in the intestines.

Page 1

Nutrition and medication together helped Keeper's stools return to their normal consistency, and helped her once again, perform as a top fly ball competitor.

KAREN TAYLOR

DAR BAUMAN

JOCELYNN JACOBS

Vitamins and Minerals:
Practical Application to Performance Dogs

What you will know after reading this chapter:

· Why fat soluble vitamins are called "fat soluble"

· What tocopherols are

· If vitamin C can prevent certain bone diseases

· How vitamins enhance the immune system

· What beta-carotene is and its importance for the immune system

· Breed specific nutritional deficiency problems

We all like to think we are doing the best for our performance dogs, so what about supplements? There are hundreds of vitamin and mineral supplements on the market. Should you be using them?

Commercially prepared dog foods are usually balanced and rarely are deficient or excessive in vitamins or minerals. So as long as you are feeding a high quality, highly digestible food, chances are you don't need to use supplements. However, if you are feeding your performance dog a homemade or combination diet, excess or deficiencies of vitamins or minerals could be possible and supplements may be necessary. Additionally, some breeds of dogs have specific genetic problems that can interfere with absorption or utilization of vitamins or minerals. They too may be good candidates for supplements.

VITAMINS

Vitamins are classified into two groups: fat-soluble vitamins and water-soluble vitamins. Fat soluble vitamins include A, D, E, and K. These vitamins require fat to help them cross intestinal cell membranes. Water-soluble vitamins include the B-complex vitamins composed of thiamin (B1), riboflavin (B2), niacin, pyridoxine (B6), pantothenic acid, biotin, folic acid, cobalamin (B12), cholineitamin, and vitamin C (ascorbic acid).

JOCELYNN JACOBS

Fat-soluble Vitamins
Vitamin A

Vitamin A is important for vision, bone growth, reproduction, and maintenance of skin and epithelial tissues. It also is important for proper health of mucous membranes that line the intestinal and respiratory tracts. Vitamin A comes from both animal sources (such as egg yolk, fish liver oil, liver and milk) and plant sources.

Carotenioids, synthesized by plant cells, is another source of vitamin A for dogs. Of the carotenioids, beta-carotene is the most plentiful and has the highest activation level.

Research as recently shown that beta-carotene plays an important role in keeping the dog's immune system healthy to combat disease and injury.

Vitamin D

Vitamin D is important for normal bone development and maintenance, and it helps to regulate calcium and phosphorus absorption and metabolism. Vitamin D can be ingested orally and absorbed through the skin upon exposure to sun – a source of UV light. It can be stored in the liver, muscle, and fatty tissue for future use.

Beta-carotene – Boost to the Immune System

It is well known that stress affects the immune system. Performance dogs experience more stress than most dogs and may have a higher risk of contracting various illnesses. So anything that may stimulate the immune system to work better for the performance dog should be considered. Beta-carotene is one vitamin that my help to do just that.

Beta-carotene is in the family of carotenoids. Carotenoids are the dark red pigments that provide orange or deep yellow color to many plants and vegetables such as carrots or corn. Even green vegetables contain carotenoids, but their color is masked by the deep green color of chlorophyll. Dogs can not make beta-carotene, so it must be eaten or taken as a supplement.

Until recently, the role of beta-carotene and the immune system of dogs was poorly understood. In fact, it wasn't even known how well beta-carotene was absorbed by dogs' intestinal tract. Research now indicates dogs supplemented with it absorb and use it well. Also dogs supplemented with beta-carotene over long periods had better absorption than those dogs supplemented only once.[1]

Dogs have an enzyme in their intestine that converts beta-carotene into an *active* form of vitamin A. That is why beta-carotene is called a precursor to vitamin A.

Vitamin A is extremely important to produce and maintain healthy skin and membranes lining the respiratory and intestinal tract. The skin and lining of the respiratory and intestinal tract are important first lines of defense against foreign bacteria and viruses. So dogs fed diets with beta-carotene may have stronger immune systems than those who are not.

Beta-carotene also has been shown to significantly increase the functioning of B and T lymphocytes, cells that play an important role in combating infection. Dogs supplemented with beta-carotene have significantly higher levels of antibodies (by producing B cells) than dogs fed diets without beta-carotene.[1] So beta-carotene may be one of the keys to helping dogs stay healthy and competitive longer.

Vitamin E

Vitamin E is a potent antioxidant. Antioxidants prevent oxidation which destroys and injures normal tissues. Tocopherols (a type of vitamin E) are commonly used as natural preservatives in dog foods to stop oxidation of fat and prevent rancidity.

Likewise, vitamin E stabilizes lipids (fat) of cell membranes of organs and tissues in the body. In general, the higher the fat content in a diet, the more vitamin E is required to counteract the normal oxidation processes and metabolism of fat. Vitamin E is found in wheat germ, corn oils, soybean oil, sunflower oils, and cottonseed oils. Most animal food sources (such as egg yolk and dairy products) supply very limited amounts of vitamin E.

The liver has large amounts of vitamin E, but it is also found in most all tissues of the body.

Vitamin K

Vitamin K's most important function is to help blood clot. Vitamin K is required for production of four clotting factors (prothrombin and clotting factors VII, IX, and X) in the liver. Vitamin K is found in leafy green vegetables such as spinach, kale, cabbage, and cauliflower. Liver, egg, and certain fish meals also contain vitamin K, but at lower levels.

Certain forms of vitamin K are synthesized by bacteria in the large intestine, and this contributes to at least some, if not all, of the daily requirement for dogs. Dogs with intestinal problems or those treated with certain antibiotics will have lower bacterial counts in the large intestine – these dogs may have an increased need for supplements of vitamin K.

Water-soluble Vitamins
Vitamin B-complex

Vitamin B-complex consist of thiamin, riboflavin, niacin, pyridoxine, pantothenic acid, biotin, folic acid, cobalamin, and choline. All nine act as ***coenzymes*** (chemical "helpers" for chemical reactions to occur) for energy metabolism and tissue synthesis. Folic acid, cobalamin, and choline are particularly important for growth, cell maintenance, and blood cell production. The other five are important in energy metabolism.

Vitamin C

Humans, guinea pigs, and a few other species can not make vitamin C. Deficiencies of vitamin C in these species result in a condition called ***scurvy*** which causes impaired wound healing, capillary bleeding, anemia, and abnormal bone formation. Dogs, on the other hand, can produce vitamin C,

JOCELYNN JACOBS

Vitamin Deficiencies and Excess[2]

	Deficiency	Excess*
Vitamin A	Impaired growth, reproductive failure, loss of skin integrity, other skin conditions	Skeletal abnormalities
Vitamin C	Not required by dogs	Non-toxic
Vitamin D	Rickets, osteomalacia, nutritional secondary hyperparathyroidism	Excess calcium in blood, bone resorption, soft-tissue calcification
Vitamin E	Reproductive failure	May increase vitamin A & D requirements
Vitamin K	Increased clotting time, hemorrhage	None recorded
Biotin	Skin abnormalities	Non-toxic
Choline	Neurological dysfunctions, fatty liver	Diarrhea
Cobalamin	Anemia	Non-toxic
Folic Acid	Anemia, low white blood cell counts	Non-toxic
Niacin	Black tongue disease	Non-toxic
Panthothenic acid	Anorexia, weight loss	None recorded
Pyridoxine	Anemia	None recorded
Riboflavin	Nervous system dysfunctions, skin abnormalities	Non-toxic
Thiamin	Nervous system dysfunctions, anorexia, weight loss	Non-toxic

*Where non-toxic is listed, this is for moderate excesses. At extremely high doses, there may be a possibility of some side effects, but it is unknown at what levels they are.

and do not have a daily requirement for it. Dogs produce vitamin C in the liver from glucose and galactose metabolism.

Some breeders and performance dog owners add vitamin C to their dog's diets because they believe it prevents certain developmental bone and skeletal problems. Some others supplement their dogs with vitamin C during growth, stress, and illness dogs because they believe the dog doesn't produce sufficient vitamin C or their dog may have a higher requirement for it. Currently there is little research proving supplemental vitamin C is beneficial for any of these situations. However, daily use of moderate doses (500-1,000 mg) is probably not harmful.

MINERALS

Calcium and Phosphorus

Because these two minerals work hand-in-hand, they will be discussed together. Calcium and phosphorus are important components of bone and teeth. Both are critical for skeletal integrity, and both can be reabsorbed from bone and transported by the blood to other sites in the body when needed. Hormones and other body chemicals help keep the balance between the two.

The recommended ratio of calcium to phosphorus for dogs is between 1.2:1 to 1.4:1. By supplementing calcium, this ratio will become unbalanced, throwing regulating systems in the body off while creating problems especially for young dogs. In young, quickly growing puppies, supplementing calcium alters the calcium to phosphorus ratio and developmental skeletal problems such as osteochondrosis, hypertrophic osteodysptrophy, hip·dysplasia, and panosteitis can occur. Some breeders believe that large breed puppies require more calcium than smaller breed puppies, and supplement it during the growing phase. When this is done, not only is the ratio altered, but also the absolute levels of calcium increases creating many developmental skeletal problems.[3]

Commercial dog foods are required to have the proper ratio and recommended levels of calcium and phosphorus. If you are feeding a homemade or combination diet, determining what the ratio of calcium to phosphorus is and the absolute amount of calcium is difficult to assess. Ideally homemade and combination diets should be sent to a nutrition laboratory (university or independent nutrition lab) on a regular basis to analyze the content of these and other minerals. If this isn't done regularly, it is possible to cause developmental skeletal problems especially in growing large breed dogs.

Many general multi-vitamin and mineral supplements made for dogs may have high levels calcium (since it generally is a very cheap mineral and frequently is used as a filler) without regard to the ratio of calcium to phosphorus. By supplementing dogs with many of these products, both the ratio of calcium and absolute amounts may alter the delicate balance between these two minerals creating health problems.

Calcium is found in high levels in diary products and vegetables. Grains, meat, and organ tissues have smaller levels of calcium. Phosphorus is found in a large variety of meat foods such as fish, poultry, beef, and organ meats.

Cobalt

Cobalt is part of vitamin B12. Cobalt is found in diary products and fish.

Copper

Copper and iron are two minerals that have a synergistic relationship. Copper must be present for iron to be absorbed from the intestine and transportation to body tissues. Copper is also important in the production of hemoglobin. Copper is stored in the liver which is why organ meats, such as liver, provide a high amount of copper in a diet.

Iodine

Thyroid hormones such as thyroxine and tri-iodothyronine contain the mineral iodine. Animals with a deficiency of iodine have enlarged thyroid glands and a deficiency of thyroid hormones. Growing animals with iodine deficiencies can have poor growth, skeletal deformities, skin abnormalities, as well as neurologic disorders. Iodine is found in meats such as fish, beef, and liver, so a dietary deficiency of iodine is unusual in dogs.

Iron

Iron can be found in just about any cell of the dog's body, but the highest concentration is in red blood cells as hemoglobin and myoglobin. Hemoglobin helps transport oxygen from the lungs to the tissues through the bloodstream. Meat by-products such as liver and kidney are the richest in iron. Other types of meats, eggs, fish, whole grains, and vegetables also contain iron.

Magnesium

Magnesium is important to provide structure to the skeleton and for proper nerve impulses and muscle contractions. It is found in foods such as grains, vegetables, and diary products.

Manganese

Manganese plays an important role in normal cell functions such as metabolic reactions and regulation of nutrient metabolism. It also is important for reproduction and normal bone growth. Whole grains and vegetables are good sources of manganese. Meat and other animal based products contain very little manganese.

JOCELYNN JACOBS

Mineral Deficiencies and Excess[2]

	Deficiency	Excess
Calcium	Rickets, oesteomalacia, nutritional secondary hyperparathyroidism	Poor skeletal development, leads to other mineral deficiencies
Cobalt	Dietary deficiency unlikely, vitamin B12 deficiency, anemia	Unknown
Copper	Anemia, poor skeletal growth	Inherited copper disorder causes liver disease
Iodine	Dietary deficiency unlikely, goiter growth retardation, reproductive failure	Dietary excess unlikely, goiter
Iron	Anemia	Dietary excess unlikely, absorption regulated by dog's needs
Magnesium	Soft-tissue calcification, enlargement of long bone growth plates, neuromuscular irritability	Dietary excess unlikely, absorption regulated by dog's needs
Manganese	Dietary deficiency unlikely, poor skeletal growth, reproductive failure	Dietary excess unlikely
Phosphorus	Same as calcium deficiency	Causes calcium deficiency
Selenium	Dietary deficiency unlikely, skeletal & cardiac abnormalities	Dietary excess unlikely, heart problems muscle conditions, liver & kidney
Sulfur	Not reported	Not reported
Zinc	Certain skin problems, hair depigmentation, growth retardation, reproductive failure.	Causes calcium & copper deficiencies

Selenium

Selenium is an important part of an antioxidant enzyme that protects cell membranes. Good dietary sources of selenium include fish, meats, and grains. Because selenium is so abundantly found in most foods dogs eat, supplementation is rarely needed and, in fact, supplementation can be toxic.

Sulfur

Sulfur is used for the synthesis of cartilage, insulin and heparin (an anticoagulant). It is an important component of sulfur-containing amino acids such as methionine and cystine. It is found in most meats.

Zinc

Zinc is important for normal fat, protein, and carbohydrate metabolism. It also plays an important role in the synthesis of RNA and DNA, the genetic building blocks of cells. Meats, organs, milk, egg yolks all contain zinc. Some vegetables also contain zinc, however dogs absorb zinc more readily from meat and eggs.

BREED-SPECIFIC VITAMIN AND MINERAL DISORDERS

Because of both human intervention and nature's natural selective process, certain breeds have developed conditions that prevent normal absorption or metabolism of particular vitamins or minerals.

Zinc Malabsorption

Two unique conditions exist with zinc problems in dogs. The first problem is referred to as zinc-responsive dermatosis. It is not caused by a deficiency of zinc in the diet, but rather the intestines do not absorb enough zinc even though there is adequate amounts in the diet.

Dogs with zinc-responsive dermatosis develop crusty, scaly skin and have hair loss around the eyes and nose. Sometimes other parts of the body such as the elbow, scrotum, prepuce, and vulva can have lesions as well. Supplementation with zinc usually results in a rapid resolution of the skin problems, usually in one to two weeks.

The Northern breeds, such as Siberian Huskies and Alaskan Malamutes have a higher incidence of zinc responsive dermatosis. Stressful conditions, such as racing, showing, pregnancy/lactation, appear to worsen the condition. Dogs that are healthy and not stressed appear normal, but under stressful situations, the condition arises. Zinc responsive dermatosis tends to run in families and can be passed down to offspring and future generations. The mode of inheritance is unknown. Other breeds such as Great Danes and Doberman Pinchers also have been reported to suffer from this condition.

A second zinc condition occurs in Bull Terriers – it is a form of zinc malabsorption. It is called *lethal acrodermatitis* and it can be deadly. It is an autosomal recessive trait and affected dogs are unable to absorb zinc even when the diet is supplemented with very high levels. These dogs can develop immunodeficiencies, have stunted growth, and severe skin lesions by 10 weeks of age. Most rarely live past 7 months.

Copper Storage Disease

Although copper storage disease occurs most commonly in Bedlington Terriers, it also has been reported to affect Doberman Pinchers, West Highland White Terriers, and Cocker Spaniels. It is caused by an autosomal recessive gene in Bedlington Terriers, but its mode of inheritance in other breeds has not yet been determined.

In copper storage disease, removal of copper from the liver is impaired which causes copper to be built up in the liver. This eventually results in liver malfunction and disease.

Malabsorption of Vitamin B12 in Giant Schnauzers

Dogs that suffer from a deficiency of vitamin B12 develop anemia and neurologic deficits. This is because vitamin B12 plays an important role in several cellular reactions, and for the formation of DNA and red blood cells. Dogs affected by vitamin B12 malabsorption problems exhibit poor growth, lethargy, weakness, anorexia or poor appetite, low white blood cell counts, and anemia.

The giant schnauzer is one breed that can suffer from a vitamin B12 deficiency. Although the exact mode of inheritance has not been proven at this point, it appears to be genetically transferred as a simple autosomal recessive trait. Oral supplementation of vitamin B12 is not effective in resolving the B12 deficiency in these dogs. These dogs may have a defective transport system of B12 across the intestinal cell lining. However, vitamin B12 injections intradermally will cause complete resolution of clinical signs. These dogs require vitamin B12 injections for their entire lives.

APPLICATION TO PERFORMANCE DOGS

It is critical to ensure you are feeding your dog a balanced diet when considering vitamins and minerals. More is not always better, and in fact, can create serious medical problems. Feeding a high quality, premium dog food is one way to ensure the basic vitamin and mineral needs for your dog are being met. Look for those diets that promote vitamin packages to build and maintain a health immune system.

If feeding a homemade or combination diet, assuring the proper balances of vitamins and mineral will be trickier. Regular evaluation of your diet at a nutritional lab can help determine if the proper ratios certain minerals are present, or that the vitamins are in high enough quality for absorption.

References for this Chapter

[1]Lepine, Allan. Nutritional Management of the Large Breed Puppy. In Reinhart, GA and Carey, DP, eds. *Recent Advances in Canine and Feline Nutrition Volume II.* Wilmington, OH: Orange Frazier Press, 1998; 53-62.

[2]Case, LP, Carey DP, and Hirakawa DA. *Canine and Feline Nutrition.* St. Louis, MO: Mosby-Year Book Inc., 1995.

[3]Chew BP, et al. Importance of B-Uptake and Immunity. In: *Recent Advances in Canine and Feline Nutrition – 1998 Iams Nutrition Symposium Proceedings*, 1998; pages 513-522.

Dudley and Growing Pains

Dudley was a 10 month old Newfoundland. His owner had big plans of making him their next water rescue competitor. He started his training at a young age and was doing very well. Around 9 months of age, however, his owner notice he was favoring his left front leg during training. Then a couple weeks later, it appeared the right front leg was giving him problems. Cage rest and aspirin did not seem to help.

Although Dudley seemed to be limping mostly on right front leg, he exhibited pain in both front legs around the shoulder joints when palpated by his veterinarian. Both joints were x-rayed and showed bilateral osteochondrosis – that is, both joints had pitted cartilage along the weight bearing surfaces. The right leg's abnormalities were much worse than the left shoulder's, but never-the-less, both were affected.

Dudley's veterinarian discussed options for treatment including surgery. They also discussed Dudley's diet. He was being fed a premium commercial dog food and also supplemented with 2,000 mg of calcium twice a day. This is a high enough level of calcium to affect the delicate balance of calcium and phosphorus, and may be one of the reasons for his condition.

Dudley's owner eliminated calcium supplementation, kept him on the high quality premium food, and opted for surgery on the worse of the two shoulder joints. The other joint was managed with medication and cartilage rebuilding supplements. About 4 months after surgery, he began his

Page 1

training again and did eventually become a good water rescue dog.

This case demonstrates how detrimental over-supplementation can be of certain minerals. Be careful when being conned into thinking if a little is good, then more is better when it comes to supplementation.

MARSHA STANDLER

Page 2

JOCELYNN JACOBS

MARK GILLILAND

CHAPTER 10

Water:
The Most Essential Nutrient to a Performance Dog

What you will know after reading this chapter:

· Where water is stored

· How dogs lose water

· How to know if your dog is dehydrated

· How to prevent your dog from getting dehydrated

· How much water your dog needs per day

Performance dog owners know how important nutrition is for both health and performance. They spend time evaluating pet food labels, talking about nutrition with other competitors, and seeing how well their dogs actually do on various foods. However, one thing that dog food can't supply enough of is water!

Water is an easy thing to overlook in our dog's nutritional program. However, it is essential for their health and ability to perform. Most working dogs can tolerate a dietary deficiency in protein, fats, vitamins, or minerals for a short time. It can take weeks or even months to detect any adverse effects caused by nutritional deficiencies on performance or health. However, dehydration will lead to a diminished performance quickly, and in severe cases, can even lead to death.

WATER COMPARTMENTS

Total body water content of a healthy dog is approximately 70% of its body weight. So, for a 70 pound Golden Retriever, water is responsible for 49 of that 70 pounds! Water is found in two areas: ***intracellular*** (within cells) and ***extracellular*** (outside cells). Of these two, extracellular water is easier and quicker to replace than intracellular water. That is an important concept to remember when re-hydrating your dog is the goal. In a severely dehydrated dog, even though they may appear to be re-hydrated based on physical signs (extracellular water loss is replenished), they may continue to need more fluids than anticipated to fulfill intracellular water losses.

Water Compartments of the Canine Body	
Intracellular	65%
Extracellular	35%
Total body water	100%

Intracellular Water

Intracellular water is found within each cell of the body. Approximately 65% of the body's water is found in this compartment. Water within cells is used to generate energy for the cell, to synthesize new cell components, allow transport of components within a cell, and detoxify cell waste.

Extracellular Water

Extracellular water is found outside cells but within three locations. About 20% of the body's water is in the interstitial space. Water in the interstitial space lies outside cells and bathes them. Its main role is to be a transport medium for nutrients, materials, and wastes in and out of the cells.

About 10% of the body's water is in plasma, the liquid component of blood. This liquid transports blood cells and nutrients all over the body through blood vessels.

About 5% of the body's water is found in various other locations such as aqueous humor (fluid found in eyes), synovial fluid (found in joints), cerebrospinal fluid (surrounding the spinal cord and brain), and secretions of the intestinal tract.

Under most circumstances, water is free to shift between any of these compartments depending on the needs of the animal. For example, during exercise, the metabolic changes in muscle cells stimulate water to move into the cells from the interstitial (extracellular) fluid space by the process of osmosis. That explains why weight lifters always look bigger immediately after a workout, because much of the fluid surrounding the muscle cells is drawn into muscle cells causing them to expand.

With more water being shifted from the interstitial space into cells, there is less water around the cell, so water moves from plasma to replace fluid in the interstitial space. The decrease in plasma fluid makes the dog thirsty, so the dog drinks more to replenish the lost fluid.

If exercise is prolonged and water is not available, your dog can suffer from dehydration. With reduced plasma fluid, the heart has to work harder to pump thicker blood. In addition, there is less fluid traveling through the vessels to provide oxygen and nutrients to tissues. In severe cases of dehydration and prolonged exercise, critical plasma volume loss can lead to major organ failure and even death.

WHERE WATER IS LOST

Dogs are constantly losing water through urine, feces, respiratory vapor (panting/breathing), saliva, and sweat. Of these five, only minor water loss occurs from sweating since dogs only sweat a small amount through their foot pads. Of the other four, the amount lost is dependent upon your dog's health, environment, workload, and diet.

Health problems can greatly influence the amount of water lost on a daily basis. Urinary or kidney diseases, diabetes, systemic infections, and other metabolic diseases can increase urine output causing water loss. As a result, those dogs with health problems need to have their hydration status closely monitored.

Environmental temperature plays a large part in how much water is lost through respiration. In low humidity and cool temperatures air has very little moisture in it. By the time breathed-in air reaches the lungs, it is saturated with water, and nearly 6% of every exhaled breath is

Water is water, right?

Well it may seem that way, but to dogs (and even to many of us owners!) not all water is created equal – at least taste wise! There is city water, well water, treated water, untreated water, bottle water, carbonated water, and the list goes on and on. All have their own taste, and some are more palatable than others. The best bet to keep your dog drinking (especially while at a performance event) is to bring your own water from home. Most dogs won't drink water that is unfamiliar to them, and keeping these dogs hydrated at an event or show can be difficult. So, in terms of taste at least, not all water is created equal.

water. In warm and humid temperatures, inhaled air is nearly saturated with water, so your dog loses less water from the lungs with each breath. However, in warm, humid temperatures, dogs tend to pant more to cool themselves off, which increases water lost through salivation. Thus, water losses in warm conditions are equal or greater than those seen in cold, dry environments.[1]

Exercise also plays a major role in the amount of fluid lost. For example, a 45 lb couch potato dog living in a climate controlled environment loses about 1000 ml of water through its urine, about 100 ml of water through its feces, and 300 ml of water through evaporation from breathing and salivating in a day. However, if that same dog was moved outside and required to run a long distance sled race, he would lose about 2250 ml of water through urine, 250 ml through the feces, and 2000 to 2500 ml from breathing during exercise!

Lastly, diet also plays an important role in water loss. Dogs fed poor quality foods need to eat more to meet energy and nutrient needs. Increase in food consumption causes an increase in fecal (stool) output. With feces being 80 - 90% water, this means dogs fed poor quality diets (and thus higher stool production) have a significant loss of water through feces each day. More food also means more production of metabolic wastes which must be filtered and excreted by the kidneys – another loss of water. So, feeding a high quality performance food to these dogs will help decrease the amount of water loss on a daily basis.

When does my dog need more water – when it is hot or cold?

Dogs should be offer fresh, clean water as often as possible. All performance dogs need and will drink more water than the average house dog. You will find, however, that performance dogs usually need more water when it is warm or hot because of increase water loss through respiration. Dogs that are hot pant more. Panting causes increase loss of water through exhaled air which in turn increases the need for water.

Just because it is a cold day, however, don't feel as if you don't need to offer your dog water! If your dog is working they probably are panting, and that still means water loss through respiration.

DEHYDRATION

Hydration of working and performing dogs is critical. If not properly hydrated your agility dog will have less energy, less focus, and poor overall response times. Thus, recognizing if your dog is dehydrated, what to do if you

think they are, and how to
prevent it are very important
to ensure the best possible
performance of any working
dog.

Recognizing Dehydration

Recognizing a dehydrated
dog is key since early
recognition allows your dog
the best chance for a rapid
recovery. Dehydration can be categorized (based on signs your dog
demonstrates) as mild, moderate, and severe. Mildly dehydrated dogs may
appear to be more sluggish and less focused on the task at hand. Sometimes a
change in behavior may be the only thing you notice. For example, a normally
mild mannered dog might growl or act aggressive toward another dog as he tries
to say, "Leave me alone – I don't feel well." Physically, his skin may tent (see
sidebar) being slow in its return to a flatten position.

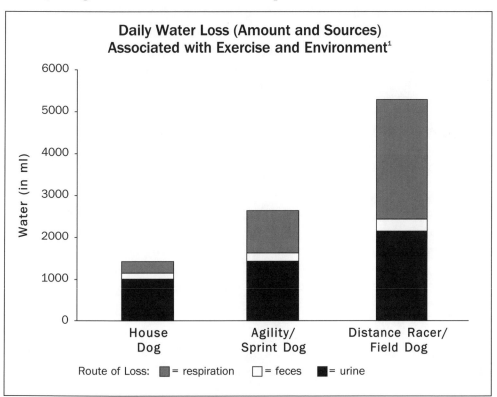

Moderately dehydrated dogs may refuse to work or exercise. They may have severely labored panting, and begin to have a dull look to their eyes. They may seem preoccupied and appear not to hear you when you talk or pet them. Curiously, most dogs will refuse to drink or take treats when moderately dehydrated.

Severely dehydrated dogs are a medical emergency. These dogs are very lethargic and may be found laying on their side, unable to move. Their eyes may appear sunken into their skull, and a dull look is even more pronounced. Most in this state have stopped panting to conserve water and energy just to survive. They will not eat or drink. They may appear to be in a coma like state, unable to respond to your voice or commands. Pinching the skin on dogs in severe dehydration takes many seconds if not a full minute to return to a flatten state.

What does "tenting of the skin" mean?

When dogs are moderately to severely dehydrated, fluid levels in the skin are decreased. Thus, when pinching the skin over the neck or back, the skin may stay up or pinched (looking like a tent) rather than immediately drop to its normal flat position as seen with well-hydrated dogs.

If your dog is mildly or moderately dehydrated, his skin may slowly drop back into place over a few seconds. Severely dehydrated dogs have skin that takes over 3-5 seconds to return to place or may stay in the tented position even longer. These dogs are in desperate need of hydration and may be close to death. Immediate medical assistant is critical!

Physical signs of dehydration
- Refusal to exercise or work
- Poor focus on the task at hand
- "Tenting" of the skin
- Refusal to drink or take treats
- Lethargy
- Dull look to the eyes
- Severely labored breathing (except in severe dehydration where panting ceases to conserve water and energy)
- Sunken eyes into the skull
- Inability to move (severe dehydration)

Treating Dehydration

Mild and sometimes moderate dehydration can usually be treated by having the animal drink to replace lost fluids. However, as moderate dehydration progresses or becomes severe, the animal's own ability to correct its problem diminishes. Most dogs in late moderate to severe stages will refuse to eat or drink. They need immediate veterinary care for administration of fluids. Moderately dehydrated dogs can be given subcutaneous or intravenous fluids to help replace fluid loss. Severely dehydrated dogs are medical emergencies, and a high priority is giving intravenous fluids to replace fluid loss as quickly as possible. Dogs with severe dehydration can easily die from organ failure.

Preventing Dehydration

To prevent dehydration, dogs must drink enough water to replace that which is lost. Most dogs will do this on their own if water is provided at all times. When a dog is fed a dry dog food thoroughly soaked in water, 70-80% of what is ingested may be water. The rest of the water taken in comes from drinking water. In the case of sled dogs or many outside dogs, some will eat snow or ice to meet their water needs. A small amount of water is also generated by cells of the body when converting fats, carbohydrates and proteins into energy. For each 100 kcal of energy burned, about 13 ml of water is generated.

HOW MUCH WATER DO DOGS NEED?

It is impossible to calculate exactly how much water is required by any individual dog. So you can't just provide your dog with the exact amount of water he needs per day. Instead, Mother Nature

Should I add water to my dog's dry dog food?

The answer to this question depends on many things. Before answering this question though, lets look at why some people add water to their dog's dry food. First, some add water to their dog's food because their dog eats too fast. These owners add water and then serve it immediately, not allowing the kibbles to soak up water. When water is added to dry food, the dog is forced to eat slower because of all the liquid – they are forced to lap the food and water rather than inhale the dry kibble alone.

Secondly, some people add water to their dog's food when they don't think their dog is drinking enough. Some dogs are not big water drinkers, and for some performance dogs that can be a problem. Thus, by adding water to the food (either food soaked in water or water added and served immediately), they are assured their dog is getting at least some water each day.

Thirdly, some people add water to their dog's dry food to make the meal more like a mush or gravy type meal. Frequently these people use warm water and mix the food well, allowing the dry food to soak up the water. This may make the food more acceptable to some dogs, especially if they have jaw or tooth pain.

So to answer the question, should you add water to your dog's food, the answer depends on why you think you may need to. If your dog falls into any of the above situations, then adding water might be a good idea.

has provided internal mechanisms to stimulate dogs to drink when hydration status is low. For example, as your dog's plasma gets more concentrated, the increased salt content is detected internally, triggering thirst. Since it takes a while for water to be absorbed from the stomach to the plasma, your dog's body does not rely on a return of plasma salt concentration to tell him to stop drinking. Instead the stretching of the stomach and drop in throat temperature signal that your dog's thirst has been quenched. Theoretically, a dog will drink as much as it needs as long as water is available when they need it. But in reality, working dogs frequently don't drink enough water.

Here is where the problem lies with keeping performance dogs well hydrated. Sometimes during performance events, water can not be offered at all times. If the dog does not drink during times it is offered, dehydration can occur. Thus, most performance dog owners do what they call *"baiting"* the water. Baiting involves adding flavor enhancers to water to stimulate the dog to drink. Crushed dog food and animal or chicken broth (low salt) are just a couple examples of what performance dog competitors may use to stimulate their dogs to drink between events or competitive heats.

Should I force my dog to drink between events or heats of a competition?

Fresh, clean water should be available to all working and performance dogs as much as possible. Most dogs will regulate how much water they need, and drink accordingly during breaks. However, some dogs become very stressed during competitions and may not drink at all. This can create a hydration problem. If your dog is one of those dogs that is not a frequent drinker, "baiting" the water may be an option after a competition to get him hydrated for the next day.

Sled dog racers have a unique problem. Dogs racing all day long have fewer opportunities to stop for water breaks. Thus, these dogs must take advantage of rest stops to re-hydrate themselves. Most mushers add water to their dog's food to ensure they are drinking. Additionally most will offer baited water after a meal to be assured their dogs feel hydrated enough. Most of these dogs are then rested for an hour or more before running again to allow their bodies to digest and absorb both the food and water they ingested. Dehydration can be seen if the owners of these dogs do not ensure proper watering opportunities.

JOCELYNN JACOBS

APPLICATION TO PERFORMANCE DOGS

Water is a very important part of keeping your performance dog in tip-top condition. Dehydration can easily lead to poor performance, or worse yet, serious health conditions if not properly addressed. Remember to always evaluate your performance dog and watch for any early warning signs of dehydration. Offer him water or baited water on a regular basis. Consult with a veterinarian if the signs of dehydration become severe – it is a medical emergency.

Can my dog drink too much?

Some dogs drink too much because of metabolic diseases or conditions, such as diabetes, kidney problems, or adrenal gland abnormalities. In these cases, they have an abnormally large thirst for water. However, for the average dog drinking too much water is only a problem if they are going to be asked to perform or work shortly after drinking. If your dog is a big water drinker, only offer a small amount of water between heats or competitive trials that take place in a single day. A belly full of water can be just as bad as being mildly dehydrated in terms of how they will perform.

Sometimes after a competition on a hot day, some dogs may try to drink an entire bowl of water in a couple minutes. That probably is not a good idea because it risks stomach distention and pain. Rather these dogs should be offered small amounts (for example, 1 cup for a large dog) of water every 15 minutes until they act satisfied.

JOCELYNN JACOBS

References for this Chapter

[1]A. Reynolds. Hydration Strategies for Exercising Dogs. In Reinhart, GA and Carey DP, eds. *Recent Advances in Canine and Feline Nutrition Volumn II*. Wilmington, OH: Orange Frazier Press, 1998; 259-267.

The Water Bucket Challenge

Chuck had been sled racing samoyeds for years. He owned 15 dogs and raced sprint races with local sledding organizations. In his kennel, each dog had their own 8 x 10 kennel complete with a dog house. He used stainless steel bowls for feeding and had plastic buckets attached to each dog's house for water.

One year he purchased a few new dogs for his team from another bloodline. He loved the way these new dogs ran on his team, but when resting in their kennels, every one of them would chew on the water buckets, dumping them in the process. Some weeks he went through as many as 5 new buckets replacing ones that were leaking because of bite marks and cracks. This new behavior was catching on to some of his other dogs and he decided this new habit had to stop!

Chuck decided if he fed the dogs with enough water during their meals in the morning and night, that probably would be enough water to satisfy them thus enabling them to remove the water buckets from the kennels. So, Chuck started to feed each dog 6 to 8 cups of water with their daily meal and removed the water buckets from his kennels.

About 3 weeks after this change, he realized one of his older females, Polly, was sick. She was not eating well, and was lethargic and inactive. He took her into his veterinarian to see what the problem might be. His veterinarian noticed that Polly was very dehydrated and not her perky self. Blood was taken to run a chemistry profile analysis, and Polly's Blood Urea Nitrogen (BUN) and creatinine (both kidney values)

Page 1

were very high. A urinalysis was done on her urine. Polly was diagnosed with kidney failure.

Polly was dehydrated because kidney failure causes animals to drink excessive amounts of water. Being offered only 6 to 8 cups of water a day with her food was not enough to meet her water needs. Some conditions and diseases cause a high requirement for daily water intake, and if not enough water is offered, the dog can get dehydrated quickly.

ANY dog (healthy or not) can become dehydrated quickly if their individual needs for water are not met properly each day, and it is hard for any dog owner to know exactly how much each of their dogs will require because of many different environmental and genetic factors. Thus, even if water is given mixed with meals daily, additional water should be offered <u>at all times</u>.

Chuck's veterinarian approached this subject and recommended trying stainless steel water buckets instead of plastic so all the dogs would have access to as much water as they needed throughout the day. Chuck followed this suggestion and all his dogs were kept well hydrated.

JOCELYNN JACOBS

CHAPTER 11

Conditioning for Performance

What you will know after reading this chapter:

- How important conditioning is

- What conditioning involves

- At what age should you start training and conditioning your dog

- How nutrition affects conditioning

- What a body condition score is

- How to determine the body condition score of your performance dog

Your two year old, healthy male show, agility, field trial, sled, or herding dog has the picture-perfect five generation pedigree, has been in training since he was months old, and has been socialized and exposed to just about every situation imaginable. He's ready to sweep up his wins and obtain that coveted title, right? Forgetting anything?

There are four major points to consider when evaluating whether a dog is destined to be a champion and ensuring he is competition-ready: genetics, health, training, and conditioning. In this particular scenario, the first three points appear to have been met. But what about conditioning? Having a well-conditioned dog is defined as having one of prime physical status – that is, they have been exercised and worked on a regular schedule to develop good cardiovascular endurance, good muscle strength and development, and have little excess fat. So with that in mind, would others refer to your dog as being well-conditioned?

CONDITIONING IS IMPORTANT

Conditioning is an important part of getting ready for any performance event. However, how well a dog is conditioned is a common oversight for many people. Sometimes so much time is spent on getting field or ring procedure down, it is easy to forget the dog needs to develop cardiovascular endurance and optimal muscle toning to be in prime condition. Marathon runners don't just spend all their training time running – they lift weights, swim and play other sports for fun to not only tone other muscles, but also to improve their cardiovascular status. Equally, our performance dogs need to be well-conditioned so they can perform at their best!

Whether your dog is a Jack Russell or a Great Dane, conditioning *does* make a difference. How many times have you seen dogs running around the conformation ring with their top lines swaying back and forth, rolling with excess fat? Or dogs that after entering the agility ring that are so winded because of lack of conditioning, they begin to wither like a dying flower? These situations occur far too often, and if you want a dog with a long competitive life as well as a competitive edge, you must consider conditioning as a step to help rise above the competition.

People may think conditioning only involves how much and how well we exercise our performance dogs. However, nutrition is also a key to a properly conditioned dog, and can make the difference between a top field trial dog, and a mediocre competitor.

ADVANTAGES OF CONDITIONING

The advantages of conditioning for enhancing ring and field presence are endless. Physical well-being, mental well-being, and endurance are just three advantages. Physically, well-conditioned dogs are trimmer with well differentiated muscle lines. The muscles of their front and rear assemblies are strong and firm. Conditioning can enhance flow of movement helping them to extend in the rear and front with more grace and less effort. Their coordination is greatly improved, and they step with confidence and power. This is one part of ensuring a competitive edge.

Dogs that are well-conditioned also have fewer injuries, and if indeed are injured, the injuries are generally less severe. This is because firm, tight muscles and ligaments keep joints and bones in place. Well-conditioned dogs also have a higher blood flow to injured tissues which enhances healing and recovery time. This allows your dog to have better performance longevity so they can compete and train weekend after weekend for many years.

Mental well-being is also a significant benefit of conditioning. People who work out, run, or exercise on a regular basis know that endorphins are released during a session of physical activity. Regular exercise can benefit your dog by helping to improve his mental health. Well-conditioned dogs are more upbeat and seem to thrive on trotting, running, or jumping. They are more easily able to deal with stressful situations or quick, unexpected events.

The third advantage is enhanced endurance – both physical and mental endurance.

At what age should I retire my dog from performance events?

Good question, but the answer isn't an easy one. The answer depends on how healthy the dog has been, currently is, and how well you kept your dog in condition throughout its life. Many herding, sled and field dogs still compete at 10 or 12 years of age as long as they have been kept physically fit, exercised and worked on a regular basis, and don't have histories of severe injuries or lamenesses. One of my own sled dogs, Pippin, raced a 26 mile race at 10 years of age in the lead position. Keep in mind, however, that she had hundreds of miles on her that Fall during the training season, and had thousands of miles on her in harness for the previous 9 years.

Aspen, also an Alaskan Malamute, is another example. He was competing at agility trials at 9 years of age. He was kept in excellent condition (through harness work on a sled team and jogging with his owner every day) and at an ideal weight all his life. He began to slow down and act stiff after competitions his 10th year, so the decision was made to retire him. He still is exercised on a regular basis, although not as rigorously.

If you want to keep your dog competing as long as possible, then right from the tender age of only a few months old, start exercising them. Over time increase the duration and level to ensure a well-conditioned dog, and keep it up throughout their lives. Lameness or joint and tendon injuries will limit the competitive lifespan of any performance dog. Keeping them in shape and well-conditioned may help to prevent injuries or long lasting lamenesses from occurring.

Conditioning enhances physical endurance of a dog through cardiovascular and muscle development. Cardiovascularly, well-conditioned dogs have more blood circulation to various muscles and organs, providing much needed oxygen and nutrients. This helps make muscles and organs function more efficiently especially during times of demanding physical stress. Well-developed and well-tuned muscles are also a benefit of highly conditioned dogs. Because muscles are the power-house of strength and endurance, if they are not in top physical shape dogs will not be able to stay competitive for long periods of time.

Mentally, waiting for his turn in large agility, flyball, herding, or field trial classes or even group competition for the conformation show dog, can be very tiring and boring. With extra environmental stresses such as heat from an inside event or constant sun bearing down during an outside event, the animal's endurance can quickly fade. However, the well-conditioned dog can appear as excited, alert and stimulated at the time of their event competition as they did the minute they arrived.

HOW TO CONDITION

So how can you ensure your dog is well-conditioned? Through exercise and proper nutrition. Both can give you the longivity you desire as well as the competitive edge your dog needs.

Exercise

A form of physical conditioning can begin as young as five or six weeks of age. Puppies run, play, and tussle with their siblings or gentle young or older dogs. Puppy play is critical for development of coordination and muscle strength. They also can be taken out into the woods or field with older, more experienced dogs and learn by sniffing and exploring new sights, sounds, and smells.

This isn't limited to medium or large breeds either. Smaller dogs can partake in similar activities. Take your dog for a run in the woods so he can learn to jump over logs, run between trees, and through little puddles. This is great for developing muscle strength and coordination, and helps with socialization.

Adult dogs can be conditioned in a variety of ways. For many of the smaller breeds, long walks or even short runs can be beneficial. Swimming is another great way to condition all sizes of dogs since it not only helps trim and tone, but develops strength and endurance.

Harness training is not just for sled dogs anymore either! Many dogs are trained in harness to pull ATV's, three or four wheeled "rigs" (carts made for being pulled behind the dogs) or modified scooters with mountain tires and brakes. Training in harness develops and builds muscle, as well as provides endurance training.

Nutrition

Nutrition is the other key to proper conditioning. Feeding a high quality, balanced dog food is important. Diets that include a highly digestible source of animal protein provide proper amino acids for dogs. Amino acids found in

At what age should I start to train and work my dog?

In general, no dog under 6 months of age should undergo strict training for an event. Instead, play time or low-stress introduction to the event is more ideal. Forcing puppies to perform before their muscles and coordination are developed or before they are mentally equipped to deal with an event can be stressful and could, in fact, create fear and anxiety. Instead, for a hunting puppy, romps through the woods and fun retrieving games are good examples of an introduction to sport. Sled dog puppies can be put in a special puppy harness to get the feel of the harness. Agility puppies can have puppy play time with agility equipment so they can sniff and play around the equipment. The key is to keep introduction to a sport light and stress free.

At 8 to 12 months of age, introduction to the sport may be increased. Hunting puppies can retrieve things from the water which takes more coordination than they had when they were younger. Sled dogs can be put on an actual sled team for short 1 mile loops with experienced dogs to help guide and give them confidence. And agility puppies may start to jump short jumps with lots of praise and encouragement from their owners.

No hard core endurance conditioning or training should take place until the dog is at least 18 to 24 months old. It is not until this time that most dogs are mentally developed or physically prepared to undergo actual training and conditioning for most performance and working events.

animal source protein are important for proper muscle development and as building blocks for many organ functions.

High quality fats are equally important. Fats are the preferred fuel source for energy for dogs, and dogs under physical and mental stress metabolize more fats to meet their energy needs.

Diets that are higher in fat have more calories per cup than poorer quality dog foods. Subsequently, you do not have to feed as much to satisfy your dog's energy or metabolic needs. But bear this in mind if your dog has a slower metabolism: your dog may need to be fed less each day or he may become obese. If you fed your dog just one percent more food a day than he needs, in a year he will be substantially overweight. Each dog has their own personal metabolic rate, so keep this in mind and adjust your dog's food intake accordingly. Also be aware how much exercise and training he is doing may increase or decrease his metabolism, and food consumption should be adjusted accordingly.

BODY CONDITION SCORES

Most people think that measuring the weight of their dog is the most accurate way to determine whether he is in good body condition. Unfortunately, this method is highly inaccurate for determining body condition since dogs vary so much in bone density and muscularity. The American Kennel Club reports standard weights for some breeds that are considered ideal for those breeds. However, many of these weight recommendations provide a large range of acceptable weights. For example, AKC standard for a male Bloodhound suggests a range between 90 - 110 pounds. However, a smaller Bloodhound weighing 110 pounds probably would be obese, and a very tall, long legged Bloodhound weighing 90 pounds might be too thin.

A better way to determine if a performance dog is in good weight for their body condition is to use a body condition scoring system. This system uses the owner's eyes and hands to evaluate if the dog is overweight, underweight, or ideal. Using a four point scoring system helps to keep this subjective means more objective. This kind of scoring system takes practice; however, over the years, working dog owners can become very good at determining whether their dogs are carrying excess weight or not.

Body Condition Scoring

Body Conditioning Score of 1 - Thin Dog
- Ribs, lumbar vertebrae and pelvic bones easily visible
- No palpable fat
- Obvious waist and abdominal tuck
- Prominent pelvic bones

Body Conditioning Score of 2 - Ideal Dog
- Ribs easily palpable, but not visible
- Minimal fat covering
- Waist easily noted when viewed from above
- Abdominal tuck evident

Body Conditioning Score of 3 - Overweight Dog
- Ribs palpable with slight excess of fat covering
- Waist discernible when viewed from above, but not prominent
- Abdominal tuck apparent

Body Conditioning Score of 4 - Obese Dog
- Ribs not easily palpable under a heavy fat covering
- Fat deposits over lumbar area and tail base
- Waist barely visible to absent
- No abdominal tuck – may exhibit obvious abdominal distention

Ideally, most performance dogs should be rated a 2 on the body condition scoring system. These dogs have a small amount of extra fat for times of high stress or serious competition over a short period, but not excess fat.

Dogs beginning the training or competition season at a score of 1 are too thin. These dogs have used up their excess fat and are using muscle protein for energy. These dogs probably have higher metabolisms, and need to be on increased amounts of a high quality performance food. Starting these dogs out a little slower in the beginning of a training season may be helpful to build up muscle and add a small amount of fat to their reserves. Once they start to fit more closely to a score of 2, they are ready for heavier training.

Dogs beginning a training or competition season at score 3 are too heavy. These dogs will be in danger of hurting themselves during a training program because of excess weight on bones and joints. These dogs need to be put on a restricted amount of a maintenance food while doing light exercise and training until they achieve a score closer to a 2. Things such as frozen green beans, canned pumpkin, puffed rice, ice cubes, or carrots (all low in calories but provide increased bulk) can be added to the maintenance food to help the dog feel fuller until a more ideal body condition is met. Once they get closer to a score of 2, they can be put on a higher quality maintenance or performance food at a moderate amount. However, because these dogs may have a slower metabolism than other dogs, they need to be exercised and trained on a constant basis to keep the extra energy from being stored as fat rather than muscle.

Dogs that score a 4: shame on their owner! These dogs probably will not be able to compete this year without some serious dieting and a regular exercise program. Do not ask them to train or compete in this shape because of huge risks of muscle, skeletal, or joint trauma. Take some time to get weight off and then start them on an exercise program that gradually increases in intensity. This will save them from potentially career-ending injuries.

For those dogs who have the ideal score of 2, these dogs are ready for a great training and competition season. They should be put on a high quality maintenance or performance food at least 2 months prior to training, and they can begin training season at a moderate exercise level with intensity increased fairly quickly. Watch and document their body condition score weekly. If they are gaining weight, cut them back a little on the amount of food being fed. If they are losing weight and getting closer to a score of 1, increase their food and re-evaluate in a week.

The same person should assess the dog's body condition score weekly and ideally, charts should be made to evaluate the dog's progress. If access to a weight scale is possible, occasionally weighing your dog can allow more accurate determination if progress is being made.

Here is an example of a body condition score chart for Bentley, an Irish Water Spaniel, being fed Heavy Hunter dog food for an 8 week time period:

Table # 2
Weekly Body Condition Scores
and Amount of Food Fed

Week #	Body Condition Score	# of cups fed per day	Body Weight
1	1	4	41
2	1	5	
3	1	6	
4	1.5	6	
5	1.5	6	47
6	2	6	
7	2	6	
8	2.5	5.5	53

Bentley appears to be at the ideal body condition score when it he is about 48/49 pounds and being fed approximately 5 ½ cups of food per day on this particular dog food. However, this is dependent on how much he is exercised (for muscularity and energy usage).

APPLICATION TO PERFORMANCE DOGS

Conditioning is critical to boost your dog's performance in the ring, field, or on the trail. Keeping tract of his body condition scores is an important part of keeping them in top condition. Through proper exercise and nutritional programs, you will be better prepared to quickly take the wins he deserves.

JOCELYNN JACOBS

Lagging Huskies

Jody owned and raised Alaskan Huskies for sled racing. She had been racing for about 8 years, and the previous year started running longer distance races with her dogs.

The past summer had been extremely hot. There were many weeks with over 90°F temperatures, and because of this, she was not letting her dogs run in the dog yard as much during the day. She found it was better to let them stay in their cool, tarp-covered kennels through the day than let them run in the hot sun, risking hyperthermia.

Finally Fall came, although it was mid-October before it was cool enough to run the dogs any distance. She had a couple big races in early January, so she had an aggressive training schedule. The dogs, however, had another plan. They were not running to her expectations during the training season. They lagged even on short runs behind other mushers' teams she normally kept up with.

Jody mentioned her frustration to another musher, and to her surprise, they mentioned they had never seen her dogs as fat as they were this Fall. Jody went through the team and rubbed them down, feeling for their ribs, and realized her friend was right – her dogs were fatter than they normally were! Because of the hot summer, the dogs were not out playing as much, thus their food intake should have been decreased to match their energy expenditure. Plain and simple, she just fed them too much over the summer and now was paying for it during the training season!

Jody cut the dogs back on their food and slowly started training, building back up to the level she was accustomed to over a few weeks. Eventually the dogs got the excess weight off, and began keeping up with other teams.

No matter what performance event your dog participates in, during the off-season, don't let them get overweight and out of shape. This can cost you weeks or even months during the training season!

JOCELYNN JACOBS

Page 2

JOCELYNN JACOBS

KAKI ALMIRALL

CHAPTER 12

Performance Dogs:
Recognizing Problems and Finding Solutions

What you will know after reading this chapter:

· What the most common causes of diarrhea are in performance dogs

· How serious a problem stress really is

· How genetics affect performance

· How to tell if your dog has good conformation

· What causes weight loss in performance dogs

· How to stimulate a picky eater's appetite

Owners of performance dog face challenges that people with ordinary house dogs normally don't face. Diarrhea, poor performance, weight loss, and poor appetite are just a few of these challenges. Recognizing when there is a problem and finding solutions are key in getting working dogs back performing at their best.

CAUSES OF DIARRHEA

With some performance dogs, diarrhea and competitions go hand in hand. When your dog has diarrhea at an event it can be both embarrassing and frustrating. Your dog may have normal, healthy stools at home, but once they arrive at an event (or after a few days of competition), their stools literally fall apart. At some events, this can cause your dog to lose valuable time because of having to relieve itself, and in some events, they can be disqualified from competing. There are many causes of diarrhea, and the main ones are discussed below.

Parvovirus

A parvovirus infection causes severe bloody diarrhea, and can be fatal if not treated. Fortunately, there are vaccines on the market that can help prevent this disease. All performance dogs should have vaccines boostered on a regular basis (as recommended by the vaccine manufacturer) to prevent spreading amongst other dogs during competitive events.

Although this may seem elementary, many people who vaccinate their own dogs do not handle the vaccines properly or give the vaccines at the recommended intervals. Thus, they put their dogs at risk even as they continue to participate in performance events, and potentially spread the virus to other dogs. It is important to follow manufacturer guidelines on how to properly handle vaccines and how often they should be given. If any dog comes down with parvovirus, dogs from the same home or kennel should not participate in competitive events until all the dogs are vaccinated, the kennel is properly cleaned, and at least a month or more has passed since the outbreak.

KELLY PRUKA

I have heard about new "strains" of parvovirus going around in different parts of the country. If my dog is vaccinated for parvovirus, will he be protected against the new strains?

Just like the influenza virus (the "flu-bug" in humans) can mutate, any virus can change over time to a slightly different strain. In the 1970's and 1980's, the CPV strain was the most prevalent. In the mid-1980's, the strain mutated, and now the CPV-2a and CPV-2b strains are the most common strains of canine parvovirus. The original strain is virtually extinct at this time. Of the two new strains, the CPV-2b strain is the most prevalent while the CPV-2a strain is seen less frequently.

Most vaccines on the market today are based on the CPV-2 strain which, in most cases, provides cross-immunity to the CPV-2a and CPV-2b strains. However, some vaccine companies only provide immunity for CPV-2b because it is the most prevalent strain.

Since the mid-1980's, the canine parvovirus strains have remained relatively stable. However, at some point, the virus may mutate again, and veterinary researchers will need to isolate the new strain and determine if current vaccines on the market provide cross-protection.

If you hear of an outbreak of parvovirus occurring after shows or performance events, make sure your dogs are up to date on their vaccines. You may even want to consider pulling your dogs from events for a few weeks to be sure they are not exposed if there actually is a new strain circulating.

Another good idea is to rotate your vaccines. That is, use different manufacturers of parvovirus and distemper virus vaccines – not the same one year after year. Since not every manufacturer uses the same strain of parvovirus to manufacture their vaccine, some vaccines may be more protective against certain strains than others.

Coronavirus and Rotavirus

Coronavirus and rotaviruses also cause diarrhea. Neither cause as severe or deadly a condition as with parvovirus infections, however, if concurrent with some other infection, they may be harder to overcome.

In the sled dog community, diarrhea is commonly seen at races. In the early 1990's, researchers collected stool samples on dogs at a sled dog race to determine the cause of diarrheas plaguing dogs at this particular race. They found that many of the samples were contaminated with coronavirus and rotavirus.[1]

Currently there are vaccines for coronavirus on the market. However, the immunity provided by this vaccine may not be 100% effective for every possible strain of coronavirus, which means some vaccinated dogs can still develop diarrhea due to coronavirus infections. There is no vaccine available for rotavirus infections, so dogs must develop their own immunity to this virus.

Bacterial Overgrowth

Bacteria is normally found in intestinal tracts of dogs. There are good bacteria, such as lactobacillus, and harmful bacteria, such as salmonella or certain strains of E. coli. Good bacteria are important because they help with digestion and provide nutrients for healthy intestinal tract lining. Harmful bacteria found in the intestines may be introduced by feeding infested or spoiled foods, or by eating bacterial-contaminated objects in the environment. Many dogs have some harmful strains of bacteria present in the intestines but don't become ill. However, during times of stress or during certain intestinal diseases, harmful bacteria counts can replicate to high levels, and can kill off or crowd out the beneficial, good bacteria. This condition is known as *small intestinal bacterial overgrowth*.

Since good bacteria are so important for digestion, absorption, and intestinal lining integrity, overgrowth of harmful bacteria can cause diarrhea. Certain viruses can also cause harmful bacterial overgrowth to occur by damaging intestinal lining and decreasing normal defense mechanisms.

There are two ways to deal with small intestinal bacterial overgrowth. One is to kill the harmful bacterial populations with antibiotics. The second way (sometimes used in conjunction with antibiotics) is to supplement the dog's diet with fructooligosaccharides (FOS). FOS is a type of fiber or carbohydrate used by the beneficial bacteria of the intestinal system, but not by the harmful bacteria. This stimulates beneficial bacteria's population to increase, crowds out the harmful bacteria, and restores the natural balance of intestinal bacteria. There are a few diets on the market that have supplemental FOS such as Eukanuba Veterinary Diet® – Low Residue for Adult Dogs™ (The Iams Company, Dayton, OH).

How common is small intestinal bacterial overgrowth (SIBO) in dogs?

SIBO is more common than most realize. In a study done in 1995, SIBO was documented in 41 of 80 dogs (51%) with chronic diarrhea, representing 23 different breeds![2] Dogs with SIBO can have many different clinical signs associated with malabsorption such as weight loss, diarrhea, flatulence (gas), anorexia, coprophagy (eating stools), and polyphagia (strong desire to eat all the time). Diagnosing dogs with SIBO can be difficult because there is no easy test to determine the levels of harmful bacteria present in the intestines. Thus many veterinarians must rule out all other causes of diarrhea before they can diagnosis SIBO as the cause of diarrhea and malabsorption.

Other Diseases Causing Diarrhea

There are many different causes of diarrhea other than viruses or bacteria. Certain types of intestinal cancer, metabolic diseases, and allergies can cause diarrhea. Inflammatory bowel disease (IBD) is a fairly commonly cause of diarrhea in performance dogs. In this condition, the bowel is inflamed and is filled with many different types of white blood cells trying to heal the intestinal lining. Although small numbers of these cells are beneficial, when there are large numbers problems can occur. The intestinal lining becomes irritated resulting in hampered digestion and absorption.

Performance dogs with mild inflammatory bowel disease can have fairly normal stools at home or during an off-season, but once they experience the stress of training or competition, they develop chronic diarrhea. Dogs with this condition usually need to be on antibiotics, special diets, and/or anti-inflammatory medication to control the problem.

Parasites

Worms living in the digestive tract of performance dogs have a detrimental effect on the dog's ability to properly absorb and digest nutrients, and this can cause diarrhea if present in sufficient numbers. Parasites do damage through two mechanisms. First, parasites physically damage the lining of the digestive tract. Because of the propulsive movements of the small intestine and the flow of ingesta, many worms attach themselves to the intestinal wall or they would be swept away with food material. This results in inflammation of the intestines, affecting its ability to digest and absorb nutrients.

Second, parasites compete with the dog for nutrients. The more worms present, the fewer nutrients available for the dog to absorb. This means dogs infected with intestinal worms have a significant portion of each meal feeding worms rather than feeding themselves! To complicate matters, if your dog is fed a poor quality food with low levels of digestible nutrients, even less nutrients will be available for him. This is another good reason to feed performance dogs the best quality food possible. If he does have worms, a higher quality food will provide more digestible nutrients to help the dog meet certain nutrient requirements.

An important point of husbandry for performance dogs is a regular worming program. A routine worming program is one that minimally targets roundworms, hookworms, whipworms, and tapeworms. There are some products on the market such as Panacur® (distributed by Intervet, Inc., Millsboro, DE) that kills multiple species of intestinal worms at once.

Two intestinal parasites that seem to cause the most problems for performance dogs are coccidia and giardia. Coccidia can be picked up at many performance and field events (usually through contact with infected fecal material), and is extremely difficult to eliminate. In general, most dogs develop a natural resistance to this parasite over time. However, during times of stress or competition, your dog's immune system may allow coccidia to over-populate in the small intestines causing diarrhea.

Giardia also can cause severe diarrhea and concurrent weight loss in dogs. It is commonly picked up by contact with infected fecal material or from drinking ponds or standing water in woods or fields. It is another parasite that is relatively difficult to eliminate especially from a kennel situation. Most dogs infected are treated with metronidizole. In the late 1990's, a vaccine was introduced by Fort Dodge that helps develop the dog's natural immunity to giardia, thus decreasing the severity of a giardia outbreak. This vaccine should be considered if giardia has been a problem with your dogs in the past or if your dogs are at greater risk of exposure.

Stress

Stress also can cause diarrhea. Increased anxiety causes the sympathetic nervous system to increase intestinal motility. When intestines move ingesta too quickly, nutrients are not absorbed properly. Dogs under stress for long periods of time may have chronic diarrhea and weight loss.

Nutrition

Believe it or not, even food can cause diarrhea. Diarrhea can occur if the dog's food is spoiled or not cooked sufficiently to kill harmful bacteria. All commercial dog foods have either a code that tells when manufacturing of the product took place or have a "Best Used By" date on the back of their bags. Always check this date before feeding a commercial dog food. In addition, if you buy large quantities of food at one time, make sure the food is kept in a cool, dry storage place free from bugs to help slow aging and racidity of the product.

If you prepare a homemade diet for your dog, there is a greater possibility of your dog's food containing harmful bacteria or becoming spoiled. If your ingredients are not fresh or the meat contains harmful bacteria, you must ensure that it is properly cooked or thrown out. If you make large batches of food and store it, there is a risk that it may become spoiled by the growth of harmful bacteria. By making small batches that are cooked thoroughly, you can prevent this from happening.

Diets that are too high in fat can also cause diarrhea. This is particularly true with diets that contain over 50% of their calories as fat. Such a diet would only be used in training or competing with long distance sled dogs. If a dog on a high fat diet develops diarrhea, feeding a lower fat diet will usually resolve the problem.

> **If my dog food company does not have a "Best Used By" date on their bag or can of food, how do I read the code to find out when the product was made?**
>
> Every food manufacturer has a different coding system. Usually this coding system will not only tell when the food was manufactured, but also the location if they have different manufacture sites.
>
> The only way to be sure the product you are feeding is fresh is to call the company's customer service number and ask how to read their code dating. Also ask them if there have been studies done to determine how long the product is good for. In general, most dry dog foods are good for approximately 1 year after manufacturing, and canned foods for 2 years. However, make sure this is true for the specific product you are feeding your dog.

CAUSES OF POOR PERFORMANCE

Has your dog's performance declined lately? To find out why, it is important to examine many different variables. Look at your dog's past performance, genetics, conformation, nutrition, health, environmental changes, training, and mental alertness to see if you can identify one or more reasons for his performance decline.

Past Performance

Always keep a record of your dog's past performance. That is past performance of *this* dog, not of its parents or siblings. Offspring are not clones of their parents (at least in this day of age). Thus, they only should be compared to themselves in terms of their performance.

If your dog's agility course times are twice what they use to be, then something has changed to cause this. Injuries, nutrition, overall health, environmental changes, training, and mental alertness all should be evaluated. If your dog does not have a long standing performance record but his performance is not what you normally would expect, things like genetics and conformation should get added to the list.

Genetics of Conformation and Instinct

Genetics can make one dog a better performer than another. Conformation, mental interest, and instincts all are genetic and can be passed from one generation to the next.

All other things being equal, dogs with better conformation, that is properly balanced front and rear leg angulation, will have the ability to run faster and longer than dogs with poor conformation. Wide fronts, straight shoulders, and unbalanced front to rear angulation can all create skeletal, tendon, and muscle stress impairing movement and efficiency. Evaluating a dog's conformation is difficult for most dog people. Seeking an outside source such as someone who competes in conformation shows to evaluate your dog's conformation and movement may be helpful to obtain additional information of whether they are suitable for your chosen performance event.

Most working and performance dogs should ***single track***. That is when they are trotting, their front and back legs converge to a line centered under their body. This allows for a more fluid gait which is more energy efficient. If a sled dog is pulling a sled in snow, it is less work for them to single track. If their back paws fall into the steps made by their front paws, they have less snow to move or plow through when trotting. Also, dogs that single track don't waste energy moving side to side, using all their muscular effort for forward motion.

If your dog has a serious conformation fault, you should carefully consider whether you want to continue to train and compete with him. Over time a serious conformational fault can cause painful arthritis of the joints, bones and back.

Correct and Incorrect Coming Movement
Golden Retriever: a. good, b. crooked front, c. bowed front, d. basewide (elbows tied in)

Correct and Incorrect Going Away Movement
Samoyed: a. good, b. cow-hocked, c. bowed rear, d. too wide

An Alaskan Malamute demonstrating balanced sidegait.
Note the balance of front and rear extension, and level
(flat) topline when gaiting.

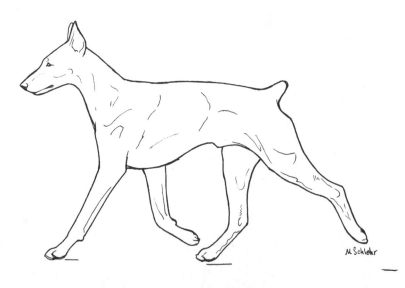

Unleveled topline (roached), and unbalanced front and rear extension.

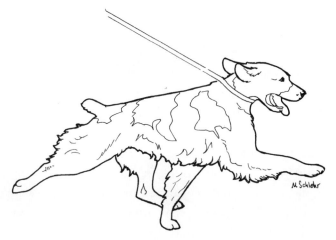

Unbalanced front and rear extension – over reaching.

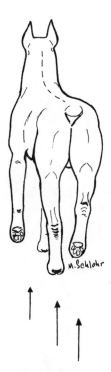

Crabbing: When viewing coming and going movement, the dog's
body should appear in a straight line. If they are slightly off,
as in this drawing, it is known as crabbing or side-winding
which demonstrate less than ideal movement.

Instinct is also genetically transferred from one generation to the next. Usually dogs that have strong working instincts pass that trait on to the majority of their pups. However, how you develop your dog's instincts is extremely important. If a hunting dog sits on the couch for the first 3 years of its life and never taken out to the field to be introduced to birds, chances are he won't turn out to be a great hunter. There are always exceptions to the rule, but in general, if you develop your dog's in-bred nature at a young age you'll help him further his instincts and become a better working dog.

When considering instincts, most think of hunting, herding, or sled dogs. However, agility and obedience dogs can have strong instincts to pass on to the next generation as well. The ability to pay attention to signals and commands, the desire to please, and mental alertness are instincts these dogs have to excel at obedience and agility. Additionally, speed and focus appear to be inherited.

Dogs that don't show interest in working or performance events should be evaluated by a veterinarian for any physical problems such as hip dysplasia and back pain, or metabolic conditions that can sap a dog's energy and lower their desire to work. If everything medically appears normal, he may not have the drive or instincts needed for that particular event.

Health

If your dog is not healthy, he will not perform at his peak. Have your veterinarian do a thorough physical examination of your dog, focusing on joints, bones and back. Consider having his blood tested, including a chemistry profile and complete blood count. Thyroid profiles are also helpful since hypothyroidism occurs in many breeds of dogs. Radiographs (x-rays) may also be considered if abnormalities are detected on physical exam.

Make sure you also assess your dog's body condition. If your dog is carrying around excess fat, he will not perform as well.

JOCELYNN JACOBS

JEANNE BEROZA

Environmental Influences

Environment can affect your dog's performance. Asking a sled dog that has been kept indoors at 70°F temperatures for months to run a race outside in below zero temperatures, is not going to perform as well as if he had been kept outside in colder temperatures.

Keeping dogs at temperatures that mimic performance situations is best. If your dog is kept in air conditioning all day while you are away at work and then asked to compete at an agility trial outside on the weekend where it is 85°F, they may have problems acclimating to the environment and his performance may suffer.

Another condition that can cause poor performance is social stress. Dogs have a pack hierarchy, and pack disruption (such as a new dog coming into your home or being dominated by another dog) can cause significant social stress. This stress may cause a previously top working dog to faultier in training or at performance events. For example, a dog who routinely does an excellent job retrieving goes out in the marsh with another dog who is more dominant may not retrieve as well as he normally does. The same thing can happen on a sled team where a dog that normally does a great job as a lead dog is suddenly intimidated by another dog introduced to the team who is more dominant or aggressive. Social stress can be an influencing factor in performance, so keeping an eye on the pack hierarchy is important.

Training Schedule

Training is another key to keeping your dog performing at his best. If your dog is not performing as well as last year, evaluate your training schedule. Did you make sure to vary the frequency, duration and intensity of your dog's training schedule? Do you give him variety to keep up his interest? Do you give him conditioning exercises to build both strength and endurance?

Dogs given the same exercises every day get bored and don't perform or train as well. Agility or obedience dogs doing the same routine over and over can become bored. Work hard to provide variety in your training program to stimulate your dog's mental alertness.

> **On the back of my bag of dog food, it says I should feed between 4 to 6 cups of food per day to my Great Pyrenees. So, how much should I feed – 4 or 6 cups?**
>
> Most dog food companies list a suggested range to feed based on the dog's size or weight. These ranges are based on average calculated values (kilocalories per day) for a certain weight of dog. So, where should you start – at the high or low end? It is best to start at 4 cups – the low end of the range. Evaluate your dog's body condition weekly, and if he is losing weight, increase the amount to 5 or 6 cups. It is easier for a dog to gain weight than lose it.

Nutrition

Nutrition plays a big role in your dog's performance. Remember, not all performance events require the same level of effort and not all dogs perform at the same level, so a dog's diet should be tailored to his individual needs. If your dog gets skinny on a high quality performance food described as ideal for working dogs, he may need to be fed more. He also may need to have a higher level of fat in the diet to provide more energy, and a diet with high quality animal protein. Athletes need to be fed like athletes. They need to have enough energy to perform and maintain their body condition.

Dogs that are overweight do not perform their best. The most common reason for overweight performance dogs is simply being fed too much. Different dogs have different speeds of metabolism. A 35 pound Border Collie may need 7 cups of food a day to maintain his energy needs while a 65 pound Retriever may only need 3 cups of the same food to meet his needs. Genetically these dogs have different metabolic rates. Even within a breed there are differences. Certain bloodlines of Alaskan Malamutes, for example, need more food to meet their energy needs for training and performance than other lines. Humans are the same way. Some people can eat everything in sight and not gain a pound, while another just barely eats and still gains 5 pounds!

CAUSES OF WEIGHT LOSS

There are many things that can cause weight loss in performance dogs. Intestinal parasites, health problems, poor quality nutrition, under feeding, stress, and poor appetite are just a few common reasons performance dogs lose weight.

Stress can cause performance dogs to lose weight. Stress increases a dog's metabolic rate causing him to need more calories per day. Competitive seasons with multiple shows or events in a row cause stress. Your dog may enjoy competing, but traveling, changes of his routine, and actual competition itself all cause a certain amount of stress. Social stresses such as a change in pack order, schedule changes, and bitches coming into heat (stressful for both the males and the females) are other stresses that may occur at home. Again, by performing a weekly body condition check (see Chapter 11), you'll recognize when your dog is losing weight and condition right away. If you find your dog is losing weight, try to determine whether he is suffering from stress, and eliminate or alter the situation.

CAUSES OF POOR APPETITE

One of the most frustrating challenges owners of performance dogs face is when their dog refuses to eat. If these dogs are such high energy creatures, why won't they eat to fulfill their nutritional needs?

There are many reasons dogs stop eating or have poor appetites. Stress, hormonal changes, poor quality diets, illnesses, insufficient or poor quality water, and hormonal changes are just a few things that can cause dogs to stop eating.

Just as you don't feel like eating when you are stressed, dogs that are stressed also may stop eating. Dogs that have been out on the campaign trail for too long or have participated in too many performance events in a short period of time may be excessively stressed and stop eating on a regular basis. The solution? These dogs need to rest at home for at least a 3 - 4 week recovery period. They need to get into a normal, easy routine again. When a dog stops eating for more than 3 days, it is a danger signal. Performance or working dogs cannot stop eating for long periods because their metabolic needs are still very high. If they don't eat, the body will begin to break down muscles and fatty storage for energy – not an ideal situation for any competitive dog.

Males frequently stop eating when exposed to bitches in season. Keeping intact males away from bitches in heat can help keep them eating on a regular basis. This may mean leaving your female at home when she is in heat while your male is at competitions.

Intestinal foreign bodies, high fevers, systemic bacterial or viral infections, bloat, and certain metabolic diseases can all cause a dog to stop eating. If a dog who is a hearty eater suddenly stops, he needs to be seen by your veterinarian to determine the cause.

Low water intake can also cause dogs to have poor appetites. Dogs that are not hydrated properly will not eat well (and they won't perform well either). Water is required for normal digestion and absorption of food, and it is also essential for most body functions. Making sure your dog is drinking is almost as important (if not more) than making sure he is eating well.

Stimulating a dog's appetite can be difficult. Adding canned food, cooked meat, fat, or vegetable oil to normal dry dog food may help increase the palatability and acceptance. After ruling out all other potential problems, your veterinarian may prescribe short-term medications that may stimulate their appetite.

APPLICATION TO PERFORMANCE DOGS

Whenever your dog isn't performing as well as they have been or to your expectation, you must look at all the physical, environmental, and genetic reasons for this. Dogs suffering with chronic diarrhea should be evaluated for viral infections, small intestinal bacterial overgrowth, parasites, stress, other metabolic conditions, and nutritional reasons causing the problem. Dogs just not performing well should have their past performance evaluated, genetics and instinct considered, health evaluated, environment and training schedule reviewed, and nutrition considered. Other factors such as weight loss or poor appetite should also be evaluated closely to see what may be the reason for poor performance. Only when we take time to evaluate what may be going on can we resolve the problem with our dogs.

JOCELYNN JACOBS

References for this Chapter

[1]Leach JB. Race Diarrhea: Causes and Cures. *Mushing*: Jan/Feb 1993, pg 30-31.

[2]Rutgers HC, Batt RM, Elwood CM, Lamport A. Small intestinal bacterial overgrowth in dogs with chronic intestinal disease. *JAVMA*. 1995; 206:187-193.

Blue's Roadblock

Blue was a 3 year old, blue merle Shetland sheepdog owned by Annie. Annie had trained multiple shelties to be top agility dogs over the years. Blue was her new prospect. She had raised him since he was 12 weeks old, and he loved agility. She held him back from many competitions until he was 3 only because she had another dog she was heavily showing the previous 2 years. Now it was his turn since she was retiring her older dog from the agility ring.

Annie kept Blue in excellent condition – he was a perfect body condition score of 2, and had quite a bit of muscle developed in this thighs and front end. The first 6 months of competitions went great – he was sweeping up the wins, taking first place ribbons in his class at almost every competition. Then something started to happen. Blue started to refuse jumps and the A frame. Annie was shocked! This dog had never refused a jump in his life!

She decided to give him a few weeks off and just let him play at home in the back yard with some of the other dogs. That's when she realized he was limping slightly on one of his back legs. Annie took Blue into her veterinarian who decided to do xrays after a thorough examination. Her veterinarian found arthritis was starting to form around both of Blue's hocks. Her veterinarian pointed out that Blue was slightly cow-hocked in the rear which was attributing to the arthritis in both of his hocks.

Blue was put on arthritis medication and glucosamine/chrondrotins to help deal with the arthritis he was developing,

but he was not going to be the top agility dog Annie had hoped
he would be. She would have to start over with a new dog,
taking at least a year to get a new pup ready and in shape for
upcoming competitions. This time Annie would spend more
time picking out a conformationally sound dog as her next
agility dog. Even though Blue had the brains and desire to be
a top agility dog, conformational unsoundness can stop <u>any</u>
dog from performing their best.

LAURA REICH

Chapter 12

JOCELYNN JACOBS

JOCELYNN JACOBS

CHAPTER 13

Practical Label Examples

After reading this book, let's see how much you have learned by looking a few examples! This chapter has three performance dogs and how to determine if a diet is right for them.

EXAMPLE 1

Mick is a 35 pound Border Collie that works in the field all day (endurance worker) herding sheep. Is this a good diet for him?

Here are some questions you should be asking as you evaluate whether this is an ideal diet for Mick:

Protein Evaluation
1. First, take a look the ingredient panel. Is the company playing the split ingredients trick?

Yes, corn has been split into ground yellow corn and corn gluten meal. With 2 of the 3 top ingredients being corn based, it means this food is primarily made of corn. It also means that if those

Mick's Diet:
Top Runner's Choice*
Guaranteed Analysis:
Crude protein (min)............ 27.0%
Crude fat (min) 12.0%
Crude fiber (max).............. 5.0 %
Moisture (max) 12.0%

Ingredients: Ground Yellow Corn, Chicken By-Product Meal, Soy Grits, Corn Gluten Meal, Brewers Rice, Soybean Meal, Beef Tallow (preserved with mixed-tocopherols), Pearled Barley, Animal Digest, Dicalcium Phosphate, Calcium Carbonate, Salt, Potassium Chloride, L-lysine Monohydride, Choline Chloride, DL-methionine, Zinc Oxide, Ferrous Sulfate, Vitamin Supplements (A, E, B-12, D-3), Manganese Sulfate, Niacin, Calcium Pantothenate, Brewer's Dried Yeast, Riboflavin Supplement, Biotin, Garlic Salt, Pyridoxine Hydrochloride, Copper Sulfate, Thiamine Mononitrate, Folic Acid, Menadione Sodium Bisulfite Complex (source of Vitamin K activity), Calcium Iodate.
*Fictional diet

two ingredients were added together, there is even less chicken by-product meal than one would think by looking at this ingredient panel.

2. What are the protein sources in this food?

Meat proteins: Chicken by-product meal. Vegetable proteins: Corn gluten meal, soy grits, soybean meal, brewer's dried yeast.

3. What can you tell about the protein sources of this food?

Because of the large amount of corn in this diet, most of the protein is probably coming from corn, although soy is also being used (another plant protein). There is not much protein coming from animal based sources (chicken by-product meal). This is further confirmed by the ingredient panel which lists amino acids such as L-lysine and DL-methionine as supplements. This suggests that because of the small amount of animal protein, supplementation with additional amino acids was required.

4. Can you tell anything about the digestibility of the protein in this food based on its label?

No. You would need to call the customer service number to get information about digestiblity.

Carbohydrates and Fat Evaluation
1. What are the carbohydrates in this food?

Ground yellow corn, brewer's rice, pearled barley.

2. What are (is) the fat sources of this food?

Beef tallow.

Ingredient Panel Evaluation
1. Are there any other interesting things listed on this ingredient panel?

Garlic salt. Garlic most commonly is used for a flavor enhancer. Sometimes when a dog food is not naturally tasty, a company adds garlic or onion salt to enhance the flavor so the dog eats it better. In general, foods with good quality fat and protein sources such as animal fats and protein do not need flavor enhancers to increase palatability.

Calculations

1. What are the percentages of protein, fat, fiber, ash, and carbohydrates (based on a dry matter basis) in this diet?

First to convert the guaranteed analysis panel to a dry matter basis, take 100% - 12% (the amount of moisture in this product) and you get 88% – the number to be used to determine the dry matter basis.

Nutrient	% on bag	Dry matter basis %
Protein	27%	30.7% (27 ÷ 88 x 100 = 30.7%)
Fat	12%	13.6% (12 ÷ 88 x 100 = 13.6%)
Fiber	5%	5.7% (5 ÷ 88 x100 = 5.7%)
Ash	Not listed – most are between 5-8% We will use 6.5% for this example	7.3% (6.5 ÷ 88 x 100 = 7.3%)

Carbohydrate: 100 – 30.7 – 13.6 – 5.7 – 7.3 = 42.7%

So the answers to the questions are:
Protein 30.7%, Fat 13.6%, Fiber 5.7%, Ash 7.3%, Carbohydrates 42.7%

2. How much of the caloric density is coming from protein, fats and carbohydrates?

Nutrient	Percent dry Matter Basis		Atwater Factor		Caloric Density (kcal/100g dry matter)	Percent of total kcal
Protein	30.7%	x	3.5	=	107.5	107.5 ÷ 372.5x100 = 29%
Fat	13.6%	x	8.5	=	115.6	115.6 ÷ 372.5x100 = 31%
Carbohydrate	42.7%	x	3.5	=	149.4	149.4 ÷ 372.5x100 = 40%
	Total kcal/100g dry matter			=	372.5	100%

So, the answers to the questions are:
Protein 29%, Fat 31%, Carbohydrate 40%

3. Where is the majority of energy coming from in this diet?

40% of the calories are coming from carbohydrates, which means they are providing the most amount of energy when compared to protein and fat. Only 29% of the calories are coming from protein and only 31% from fat.

4. Would this be a good diet to put Mick, a day-long herding dog (endurance herding), on?

No, primarily because most of the energy in this diet is coming from carbohydrates, not fat. Ideally a hard working herding dog should have approximately 45 - 50 %of their calories coming from fats (see Chapter 7), and this diet only has about 31%.

The amount of protein in this diet is almost adequate at 29% (most endurance herding dogs should have approximately 30 - 35% of their calories coming from protein – see Chapter 6), but the primary source of protein is plant protein, not animal protein, which is not as good in quality. This food might not be naturally very tasty either since they have had to add garlic oil to enhance the flavor.

EXAMPLE 2

Bepa is pointer in the middle of his field trial season. Is this a good diet to feed him?

Here are some questions you should be asking as you evaluate whether this is an ideal diet for Bepa:

Protein Evaluation

1. When looking at the ingredient panel, has the company split any of the ingredients into smaller parts?
No.

2. What are the protein sources in this food?
Meat proteins: Poultry meal, fish meal, blood meal. Vegetable proteins: Soy flour, kibbled corn.

3. What can you tell about the types of protein with this food?
It is primarily a meat based protein source with poultry and fish meal being top on the list (no split ingredients that would lower their value). There also is some soy flour as well for a protein source.

> ### Bepa's Diet:
> ### Hunter's Dream Chow*
> **Guaranteed Analysis:**
> Crude protein (min) 34.0%
> Crude fat (min) 20.0%
> Crude fiber (max) . . . . 4.5 %
> Moisture (max) 10.0%
>
> **Ingredients:** Poultry Meal, Fish Meal, Pork Fat (preserved with mixed tocopherols), Soy Flour, Wheat Middlings, Kibbled Corn, Oat Meal, Beet Pulp, Plain Dried Blood Meal, Sodium Bentonite, Corn Oil (preserved with mixed tocopherols), Liver Digest, Potassium Chloride, Propionic Acid (a preservative), Vitamin E Supplement, Choline Chloride, Iron Proteinate, Zinc Sulfate, Manganese Sulfate, Ferrous Sulfate, Ascorbic Acid, Yucca Schidigera Extract, Copper Proteinate, Zinc Proteinate, Cobalt Proteinate, Vitamin A Acetate, D-Activated Animal Sterol (source of Vitamin D3), Niacin Supplement, Copper Sulfate, Biotin Supplement, Calcium Pantothenate, Vitamin B12 Supplement, Pyridoxine Hydrochloride (Vitamin B6), Thiamine Mononitrate, Menadione Sodium Bisulfite Complex (source of Vitamin K), Riboflavin Supplement, Cobalt Sulfate, Ethylenediamine Dihydriodide, Folic Acid, Manganese Proteinate, Sodium Selenite.
> *Fictional diet*

4. Can you tell anything about the quality of protein from this label?
No. Poultry meal is poultry by-product meal that could be either higher quality by-products or poor quality by-products, so it is difficult to tell. However, there are no additional amino acids added to this food, so the animal protein must be completely meeting the amino acid requirements for dogs. Whether the protein is digestible can not be determined by reading the pet food label.

Carbohydrates and Fat Evaluation

1. What are the carbohydrate sources in this food?

Wheat middlings, kibbled corn, feeding oat meal, and cane molasses. Beet pulp is the fiber source.

2. What are the fat sources in this food?

Pork fat and corn oil – both sources of Omega-6's.

Ingredient Panel Evaluation

1. Is there anything else interesting on this ingredient panel?

Yes. They have liver digest added (a natural protein and fat product). Also, they have added yucca schidigera extract. There have been some discussions in human medicine how yucca in a diet may be beneficial for health and well-being. Currently the significance of this has not been researched in dogs.

Calculations

1. What are the percentages of protein, fat, fiber, ash, and carbohydrate based on a dry matter basis?

First take 100% - 10% (moisture) to get the factor to use to convert to a dry matter basis which is 90.

Nutrient	% on bag	Dry matter basis %
Protein	34%	37.8% (34 ÷ 90 x 100 = 37.8%)
Fat	20%	22.2% (20 ÷ 90 x 100 = 22.2%)
Fiber	4.5%	5% (4.5 ÷ 90 x100 = 5%)
Ash	Not listed – most are between 5-8%	7.2% (6.5 ÷ 90 x 100 = 7.2%)
	We will use 6.5% for this example	

Carbohydrate: 100 – 37.8 – 22.2 – 5 – 7.2 = 27.8%

So, the answers are:
Protein 37.8%, Fat 22.2%, Fiber 5%, Ash 7.2%, Carbohydrates 27.8%

> **Important!**
> Most pet food companies have a 1-800 customer service line where you can call to get addition information on digestibility, how digestibility was tested, code reading, etc. Be sure to take advantage of this when determining which food is best for your dog.

2. How much of the caloric density is coming from protein, fats, and carbohydrates?

Nutrient	Percent Dry Matter Basis		Atwater Factor		Caloric Density (kcal/100g dry matter)	Percent of Total kcal
Protein	37.8%	x	3.5	=	132.3	132.3 ÷ 418.3x100 = 31.6%
Fat	22.2%	x	8.5	=	188.7	188.7 ÷ 418.3x100 = 45.1%
Carbohydrate	27.8%	x	3.5	=	97.3	97.3 ÷ 418.3x100 = 23.3%
	Total kcal/100g dry matter			=	418.3	100%

So, the answers are:
Protein 31.6%, Fat 45.1%, Carbohydrates 23.3%

3. So, where is the majority of energy coming from in this diet?

The majority of calories are coming from fat in this diet (45.1% compared to 31.6% for protein and 23.3% for carbohydrates).

4. Would this be a good diet for a Bepa, a field trial dog, to be on during competition?

Yes. The percentage of calories coming from fat should be around 35 - 45% (see Chapter 7), which this diet has. Also, the calories coming from protein are also within the recommended range of 30 - 35% (see Chapter 6), and most of the protein is from as animal sources. It also uses pork fat and liver digest, natural sources of fat and protein which makes the food more tasty. The only thing you can't tell about this diet is how digestible the protein is because there is nothing on the dog food label that tells us that. The manufacturer of the food could be called for its digestibility ratings to find out that information.

JOCELYNN JACOBS

EXAMPLE 3

Ty is a high energy Jack Russell Terrier who does agility trials. Would this be a good diet for him during training and competition season?

Here are some questions you should be asking as you evaluate whether this is an ideal diet for Ty:

Protein Evaluation

1. When looking at the ingredient list, has the company split out any ingredients?

Yes, chicken and chicken by-product meal. The reason they probably are doing this is to emphasize how much chicken (animal protein) is in the food which probably is quite a bit. By doing this, it emphasizes they are using both chicken skeletal muscle and chicken by-product meal.

Ty's Diet:
Get Up 'N Go Dog Food＊
Guaranteed Analysis:

Crude protein (min)............ 32.0%
Crude fat (min) 21.0%
Crude fiber (max).............. 4.0 %
Moisture (max) 10.0%

Ingredients: Chicken, Chicken By-Product Meal, Ground Corn, Rice Flour, Fish Meal, Chicken Fat (preserved with mixed tocopherols), Dried Beet Pulp, Chicken Digest, Dried Egg Product, Brewers Dried Yeast, Flax, Discalcium Phosphate, Calcium Carbonate, Potassium Chloride, Choline Chloride, Salt, Vitamin E Supplement, Ascorbic Acid, Copper Sulfate, Zinc Oxide, Ferrous Sulfate, Manganese Sulfate, Manganous Oxide, Biotin, Mono and Diglycerides, Lecithin, Rosemary Extract, Vitamin A Acetate, Calcium Pantothenate, Vitamin B12 Supplement, Niacin, Thiamine Mononitrate, Riboflavin Supplement, Inositol, Pyridoxine Hydrochloride (Vitamin B6), Vitamin D3 Supplement, Potassium Oodide, Folic Acid, Cobalt Carbonate.
Fictional diet

2. What are the protein sources in this food?

Meat protein: Chicken, chicken by-product meal, fish meal, dried egg product. Vegetable protein: brewers dried yeast.

Fat and Carbohydrates Evaluation

1. What are the fat sources in this food?

Chicken fat (source of Omega 6's) and flax (source of Omega 3's).

2. What are the carbohydrate sources in this food?

Ground corn and rice flour. Dried beet pulp is a fiber source.

Ingredient Panel Evaluation

1. Are there any other interesting things listed on this ingredient panel?

Yes. They have added chicken digest, a natural source of fat which naturally makes the food more tasty. This can be beneficial for a working dog who is stressed or not interested in eating like he should.

Calculations

1. What are the percentages of protein, fat, fiber, ash, and carbohydrate based on a dry matter basis?

First take 100% - 10% (moisture) to get the factor to use to convert to a dry matter basis which is 90.

Nutrient	% on bag	Dry matter basis %
Protein	32%	35.6% (32 ÷ 90 x 100 = 35.6%)
Fat	21%	23.3% (21 ÷ 90 x 100 = 23.3%)
Fiber	4%	4.4% (4 ÷ 90 x 100 = 4.4%)
Ash	Not listed – most are between 5-8%	7.2% (6.5 ÷ 90 x 100 = 7.2%)
	We will use 6.5% for this example	

Carbohydrate: 100 – 35.6 – 23.3 – 4.4 – 7.2 = 29.5%

So, the answers are:

Protein 35.6%, Fat 23.3%, Fiber 4.4%, Ash 7.2%, Carbohydrates 29.5%

2. How much of the caloric density is coming from protein, fats, and carbohydrates?

Nutrient	Percent Dry Matter Basis		Atwater Factor		Caloric Density (kcal/100g dry matter)	Percent of Total kcal
Protein	35.6%	x	3.5	=	124.6	124.6 ÷ 426.4 x 100 = 29.2%
Fat	23.3%	x	8.5	=	198.5	198.5 ÷ 426.4 x 100 = 46.6%
Carbohydrate	29.5%	x	3.5	=	103.3	103.3 ÷ 426.4 x 100 = 24.2%
	Total kcal/100g dry matter			=	426.4	100%

So, the answers are:

Protein 29.2%, Fat 46.6%, Carbohydrates 24.2%

3. Where is the majority of energy coming from in this diet?

Fat – 46.6% of the calories are coming from fat compared to 29.2% for protein and 24.2% coming from carbohydrates.

---

4. Would this be a good diet for Ty?

That depends. If he has a very high metabolism, this diet should be an excellent diet for him. However, if he gains excess weight while being fed this diet, he may need to be on a diet lower in fat. This diet has 46.6% of its calories coming from fat, and 29.2% from protein. Many high energy agility dogs can require between 35 - 45% of their calories coming from fat. However, if it is during the training season and Ty is not being worked and exercised on a constant basis, closer to 40% of his calories coming from fat may be more than adequate. In terms of its protein content, 29.2% is close to the 30 - 35% recommended range and should be adequate.

The key in determining whether this diet is ideal for Ty depends on his overall energy level and weekly body condition score. If he gains weight while being fed only a small amount of food each day, he needs to be on a different diet where the calories coming from fat are closer to 35%.

JOCELYNN JACOBS

JOCELYNN JACOBS

JOCELYNN JACOBS

CHAPTER 14

Performance Dog Case Examples

So how did you do on the Practical Label Examples Chapter? In this chapter, there are four examples of performance dogs with problems and how they were evaluated and treated. They may be helpful if you have a performance dog demonstrating similar problems.

Duke's History

Duke was a 4 year old, intact, blue tick hound. He had lost over 20 pounds in the last 2 months (he was 53 pounds 2 months ago, and on presentation at the vet clinic, he was only 32 pounds).

Duke's owners said his stools had been a little loose but not watery diarrhea. They have been feeding an average quality maintenance dog food (not a performance or expensive dog food). They recently increased the amount they have been feeding him because they began to notice weight loss. Duke has been acting quieter around home, and is slower when out running. He is kenneled outside and has not used for hunting for the last few months. Duke is up to date on vaccines and heartworm prevention.

Duke's Veterinary Evaluation

Physically, Duke was extremely thin with a body condition score of 1. He was mildly dehydrated, had a poor hair coat quality, and had increase (gut) sounds (which means he has rapid gut motility). Duke had no fleas or other external parasites. The rest of physical exam done by his veterinarian was normal.

Duke and severe weight loss

Here are some questions that should be considered when evaluating Duke's problem:

1. What are some of the things that could be causing Duke to lose weight?

Parasites, metabolic or intestinal diseases, cancer, poor diet or under feeding, and stress are just a few things that can cause dogs to lose significant amounts of weight.

2. What types of tests would a veterinarian do to determine what is causing Duke's weight loss?

First, a fecal or stool exam should be done. Secondly, a chemistry profile and complete blood count should be evaluated. If nothing came up abnormal on these tests, then x-rays, ultrasounds, biopsies, endoscoping, and other blood tests may be options to determine the cause of Duke's weight loss.

3. What were the results of the tests done on Duke? What was causing his weight loss?

Duke's fecal/stool sample was loaded with whipworms. Based on the results of the bloodwork, Duke was severely anemic (low red blood cell count).

Whipworms drain blood from dogs, and the large amount of whipworms Duke had in his intestines were causing his anemia. Large infestations of whipworms can cause severe weight loss, poor performance, and poor health overall.

4. How was Duke treated?

Duke was given a blood transfusion (to help treat his anemia), treated with worming medication (to kill the whipworms), put on antibiotics (to help eliminate any secondary bacterial infections in his intestines caused by the worms), and fed a high quality performance food (to help him gain weight).

Within a few weeks, Duke was feeling significantly better. His red blood cell count returned to normal, and he had gained 15 pounds. Six weeks after the initial visit, his weight was 58 pounds (up from the original 32 pounds).

A Yearly Worming Program is Important

A yearly worming program should be part of every performance dog's health maintenance program. At my clinic, over 50% of the performance dogs with severe weight loss are caused by intestinal worms infestations. Many over-the-counter (pet store) worming medications do not kill all types of intestinal worms. The best way to determine the type of worms your dog may have is to take a stool (fecal) sample in to your veterinarian yearly for microscopic examination.

Every dog (even the pet house dog) is at risk for picking up intestinal worms. However, hunting, field trial, and sled dogs may be at a higher risk because of the environment they perform in. Woods, streams, and fields may carry higher numbers of parasites and may increase the risk of infection.

JOCELYNN JACOBS

Blaze's History

Blaze was a 5 year old, castrated male Siberian Husky. His owners complained that he has had chronic diarrhea and soft stools that has worsened in the last year. They mentioned he always had softer stools since he was a puppy – it was just something they had learned to live with.

Blaze's diarrhea was worse during sledding events. He does have a history of eating stones, rocks, and tree bark whenever he is bored. According his owner, he has not lost any weight, and he acts normal. As a performer, he is a good, honest worker on his team.

Blaze is fed a good quality performance dog food all year round (based on calculated evaluations as in the first part of this chapter). His owner increases amount fed during the training and racing season to keep body condition normal. He is up to date on vaccines and heartworm prevention.

Blaze's Veterinary Evaluation

On physical examination by his veterinarian, Blaze had a body condition score of 2 which is ideal for his condition. He has normal gut sounds (motility). The rest of his physical examination is normal.

Blaze and chronically soft stools

Here are some questions that should be considered when evaluating Blaze's problem:

1. What are some of the things that could be causing Blaze to have chronic diarrhea?

Intestinal parasites, metabolic or intestinal diseases, cancer, viral or bacterial infections, foreign body obstruction (due to retained rocks or stones), and stress are just a few. It does not appear that diet is a primary cause since this dog has been on a good quality performance food for a long time.

2. What types of tests would a veterinarian do to determine what is causing Blaze's diarrhea?

First a fecal/stool examine should be examined. Doing bloodwork (chemistry panel and complete blood count) should also be considered. Xrays is also a good idea since this dog has a history of eating stones and other things in the yard. A more in-depth type of x-ray evaluation called a barium series (were the dog ingests a small amount of barium dye and a series of xrays are taken) would also be another thing to consider. An ultrasound evaluation or endoscoping may also be helpful. An exploratory surgery with intestinal biopies may also be an option in determining the cause of his chronic diarrhea.

3. What where the results of the tests done on Blaze? What was causing his diarrhea?

Initially, the stool sample, bloodwork and routine xrays were all Blaze's owners opted for, and here were their results:

Blaze's stool sample: negative (no worms)

Bloodwork: all within normal limits

Xrays: A couple of small stones were seen in his intestines, but they seemed to be passing through normally (they were passed with stool material later that day).

No more tests were performed at this point. The owners decided to have their veterinarian treat him as she saw fit. If conservative treatment did not work, then they would consider additional tests.

4. How was Blaze treated?

Blaze was given antibiotics and a prescription diet (Eukanuba Veterinary Diet Low Residue for Dogs™) made for intestinal diseases and abnormalities, and was re-evaluated a few weeks later. Blaze's stools seemed to firm up a little initially, but eventually returned to the same quality even while on antibiotics and the special diet.

5. Then what happened? Was anything else done to determine the cause of Blaze's chronic diarrhea?

Blaze's owners eventually decided to have an abdominal exploratory done where intestinal biopies could be taken.

The biopsy revealed Blaze had chronic inflammatory bowel disease. Blaze was put on long term antibiotics and anti-inflammatories, put in a concrete run kennel, and kept on the intestinal prescription food. Over time, the diarrhea/soft stools improved. Only occasionally Blaze would have diarrhea brought on by stressful situations. Overall, however, the owners were please with the progress Blaze had made with the medication and prescription dog food.

Jig's History

Jig was a 2 ½ year old, male neutered Border Collie. His owner had been frustrated because they couldn't seem to get him to gain weight. Even keeping on the weight he had was a challenge. Jig was an extremely active and anxious dog. He had a very strong herding instinct.

Jig's owners fed a "maintenance" dog food (based on an evaluation like in the first part of this chapter). His owners had increased the amount being fed to 8 cups per day. Even at that high number of cups per day, Jig continued to stay thin.

Jig is used for fly ball competitions and consistently does well. He is to date on vaccines and heartworm prevention.

Jig's Veterinary Evaluation

Jig's body condition score was 1 ½. He was on the thin side, but not so thin that he was skin and bones. His veterinarian noted his physical examination was normal otherwise.

Jig and his inability to keep weight on

Here are some questions that should be considered when evaluating Jig's problem:

1. What are some of the things that could have causing Jig's weight loss or inability to keep weight on?

Parasites, cancer, metabolic diseases, improper nutrition for the dog's metabolic rate, and stress are all things that can cause problems like Jig's. Cancer is another cause of weight loss, but this probably is not the cause of his problems because he is so young.

2. How was Jig's case approached?

A stool sample was tested and found to be negative for intestinal worms. Jig was young, extremely active and hyper, and appeared healthy in all other aspects. Before any other laboratory tests were done, his food was evaluated to determine if he was getting enough calories from fat, and that the protein content was high quality as well as highly digestible.

3. What was determined by evaluating Jig's food?

Jig was on a good quality "maintenance" food for most house dogs, but it was not adequate for his high metabolic rate.

These were the problems with Jig's diet:

1. Based on a calculated evaluation, his diet had 26% of the calories coming from protein, 25% of the calories from fat, and 49% of the calories coming from carbohydrates.

2. Most of this diet had its protein coming from plant material, rather than animal protein sources. Animal protein sources provide a wider complement of amino acids important for dog's health and nutrition.

3. This diet did not have a very high number of kilocalories per cup (only 245 kcals/cup), so the caloric density was not as high as it could have been.

Jig was switched to a high performance food with a high number of kilocalories per cup (450 kcals/cup – a more energy concentrated food), and a breakdown where most of the calories were coming from fat (45%). The protein in this new diet also came primarily from animal based proteins rather than plant protein, so protein and amino acid requirements were more adequately met.

5. How did Jig do on his new diet?

Jig is active as ever, but now is able to keep weight on while his owner only has to feed 4 cups of food a day. This diet is helping to keep him at a body condition score of 2, and his owner isn't going broke trying to feed him!

JOCELYNN JACOBS

Jenny's History

Jenny was a 7 year old spayed, Golden Retriever. Her owner stated that she had always been an excellent hunter, but recently seemed more lethargic and had a lack of interested in hunting.

Jenny had been fed a high quality maintenance food during the off-season, and put on a premium quality performance food during the hunting season (based on calculations as in the first part of this chapter). She had gained quite a bit of weight the previous 6 months (from 50 to 73 lbs) even though her owner had not been feeding her more. Her owner also thought she had looked like she aged a lot in the recent months (her facial expression looks older to him). Jenny was up to date on her vaccines and heartworm prevention.

Jenny's Veterinary Evaluation

Jenny's body condition score was 4 (overweight). Her veterinarian agreed that she looked like she has aged especially in her face since the last time she had seen her. The rest of her physical examination was normal.

Jenny and Poor Performance

Here are some questions that should be considered when evaluating Jenny's problem:

1. What are some of the things that could cause Jenny's poor performance and weight gain?

Metabolic or other health problems (such as hypothyroidism or Cushing's disease), stress, environmental changes, conformational changes or recent injuries, mental interest problems (not able to keep interest in hunting as in previous years), and overfeeding are just a few that could be the cause of Jenny's problem.

Jenny's owner was feeding a high quality food during the training season and a high quality maintenance food during the off-season, so it is possible he may be overfeeding her. However, he claims he had cut back on the amount he was feeding since he noticed she had been gaining weight.

2. What types of tests would Jenny's veterinarian do to determine what was the cause of her poor performance and weight gain?

Most veterinarians will start off running a chemistry profile panel as well as a complete blood count in a case like this to determine if there are any metabolic or organ dysfunction present. Additional blood for a thyroid panel also would be considered because of the age, history, and breed.

3. What where the results of the tests done on Jenny? What was causing her poor performance and weight gain?

Jenny's chemistry profile and complete blood count came back normal. However, her thyroid test came back positive for hypothyroidism.

4. How was Jenny treated?

Jenny was put on thyroid supplementation, and within a few weeks appeared to have more energy and her weight began to drop. Within 6 months, she started to enjoy field work again and looked more like her old self.

Are certain breeds more susceptible to hypothyroidism?

Hypothyroidism is more frequently seen in certain breeds such as Golden Retrievers, Doberman Pinschers, Irish Setters, Boxers, Old English Sheepdogs, Miniature Schnauzers, Airdale Terriers, and certain types of Spaniels. However, any breed of dog can develop hypothyroidism. It appears there is a genetic tendency for this condition.

JOCELYNN JACOBS

JOCELYNN JACOBS

REFERENCES/ADDITIONAL READING

Breed Specific Nutrition

Fadok V. (1982) Zinc Responsive Dermatosis in a Great Dane: A Case Report. *J. Am. Anim. Hosp. Assoc.* 18: 409-414.

Fyfe, J., Jezyk P., Giger U., et. al (1989) Inherited Selective Malabsorption of Vitamin B12 in Giant Schnauzers. *J. Am. Anim. Hosp. Assoc.* 25: 533-539.

Jezyk P., Haskins, M., McKay-Smith W., et al. (1986) Lethal Acrodermatitis in Bull Terriers. *J. Am. Vet. Med. Assoc.* 188: 833-839.

Johnson, G. Inheritance of Copper Toxicosis in Bedlington Terriers. (1980) *Am. J. Vet. Res.* 41: 1865-1866.

Kunkle, G. (1980) Zinc Responsive Dermatoses in Dogs. In *Current Veterinary Therapy VII: Small Animal Practice*. W. B. Saunders.

Miller Jr, M. Nutritional Considerations in Small Animal Dermatology. (1989) *Vet. Clin. North Am. Sm. Anim. Pract.* 19: 497-511.

Thornburg, L., Polley, D., Dimmitt, R. (1984) The Diagnosis and Treatment of Copper Toxicosis in dogs. *Can Pract.* 11: 36-39.

Diarrhea

Leach III, J. (1993) Race Diarrheas: Causes and Cures. *Mushing.* January/February: 30-31.

General Information

Guyton, A. (1986) *Textbook of Medical Physiology*. W. B. Saunders.

General Nutrition

Burger, I. (1993) *The Waltham Book of Companion Animal Nutrition*. Pergamon Press.

Case, L., Carey, D., Hirakawa, D., Daristotle. (2000) *Canine and Feline Nutrition*. Mosby Books.

Reynolds, A. (1993) What's In the Bag? *Mushing.* September/October: 30-33.

The Iams Company. (1994) Topics in Practical Nutrition. Volume 4: number 2.

Wills, J., Simpson, K. (1994) *The Waltham Book of Clinical Nutrition of the Dog and Cat*. Pergamon Press.

Kidney Nutrition

Finco DR, Crowell WA, Barsanti JA, Effects of three diets on dogs with induced chronic renal failure. *American Journal of Veterinary Research*, 1985, 46:646-652.

Finco DR, Effects of dietary components on progression of renal failure. Proceedings of the 10th Annual Veterinary Medical Forum (ACVIM), 1992, 460-462.

Parasites

Georgi, J. (1985) *Parasitology for Veterinarians*. W. B. Saunders.

Ivens, V., Mark, D., Levine, N. (1978) *Principal Parasites of Domestic Animals in the United States.* Printed by U of Illinois Veterinary School, Champaign, Illinois.

Performance Dog History

Grandjean, D. (1998) Origin and History of the Sled Dog. *In Canine Sports Medicine and Surgery.* W. B. Saunders.

Guccoine, G. (1998) Origin and History of Racing Greyhound and Coursing Dogs. In *Canine Sports Medicine and Surgery.* W. B. Saunders.

Jennings Jr., P. (1998) Origins and History of Security and Detector Dogs. In *Canine Sports Medicine and Surgery.* W. B. Saunders.

McCartney, E., McCartney K. (1998) History of Competitive Upland Game Bird and Retriever Dogs. In *Canine Sports Medicine and Surgery.* W. B. Saunders.

Stanley, A. (1998) Origin, History, Training, and Utilization of Search, Rescue and Tracking Dogs. In *Canine Sports Medicine and Surgery.* W. B. Saunders.

Performance Dog Nutrition

Davenport GM et al. Effect of diet on hunting performance of English Pointers. Veterinary Therapeutics, Vol 2, No. 1, 2001.

Grandjean,D. (1998) Nutrition for Sled Dogs. In *Canine Sports Medicine and Surgery.* W. B. Saunders.

Grandjean, D., Paragon, B. (1992) Nutrition of Racing and Working Dogs. Part I. Energy Metabolism of Dogs. *Sm. An. Compendium* 14: 1608-1615.

Grandjean, D., Paragon B. (1993) Nutrition of Racing and Working Dogs. Part II. Determination of Energy Requirements and the Nutritional Impact of Stress. *Sm. An. Compendium* 15: 45-56.

Grandjean, D., Paragon B. (1993) Nutrition of Racing and Working dogs. Part III. Dehydration, Mineral and Vitamin Adaptations, and Practical Feeding Guidelines. *Sm. An. Compendium* 15: 203-211.

Hinchcliff, K., Olson, J., Crusberg, C., Kenyon, J., Long, R., Royle, W., Weber, W., Burr, J. (1993) Serum Biochemical Changes in Dogs Competing in a Long-distance Sled Race. *J. Am. Vet. Med. Assoc.* 202: 401-405.

Hinchcliff, K., Piercy, R, Baskin, C., DiSilvestro, R., Reinhart, G., Hayek, M., Chew B. (2000) Oxidant Stress, Oxidant Damage, and Antioxidants: Review and Studies in Alaskan Sled Dogs. In *Recent Advances in Canine and Feline Nutrition Volume III: 2000 Iams Nutrition Symposium Proceedings.* Orange Frazer Press.

Hinchcliff, K., Reinhart, G., Reynolds, A., Swenson, R. (1998) Exercise and Oxidant Stress. In *Recent Advances in Canine and Feline Nutrition Volume II: 1998 Iams Nutrition Symposium Proceedings.* Orange Frazer Press.

Kohnke, J. (1998) Nutrition for the Racing Greyhound. In *Canine Sports Medicine and Surgery.* W. B. Saunders.

Kronfeld, D., Ferrante, P., Grandjean, D. (1994) Optimal Nutrition for Athletic Performance, with Emphasis on Fat Adaptation in Dogs and Horses. *J. Nutr* 124: 2745S-2753S.

Querengaesser, A., Iben, C., Leibetseder, J. (1994) Blood Changes During Training and Racing in Sled Dogs. *J. Nutr.* 124: 2760S-2764S.

Reinhart, G. (1998) Nutrition for Sporting Dogs. In *Canine Sports Medicine and Surgery.* W. B. Saunders.

Reynolds, A. (1994) Balancing Minerals. *Mushing.* January/February: 29-32.

Reynolds, A. (1993) Figuring Out Fats. *Mushing,* May/June: 10-12, 32.

Reynolds, A. (1992) High-fat vs. High-carbohydrate Diets: How Do They Compare? *Mushing,* May/June: 22-25.

Reynolds, A. (1993) The Importance of Protein. *Mushing.* March/April: 27-29.

Reynolds, A., Fuhrer, L., Dunlap, H., Finke, M., Kallfelz, F. (1994) Lipid Metabolite Responses to Diet and Training in Sled Dogs. *J. Nutr.* 124: 2754S-2759S.

Reynolds, A., Reinhart, G. (1998) The Role of Fat in the Formulation of Performance Rations: Focus on Fat Sources. In *Recent Advances in Canine and Feline Nutrition Volume II: 1998 Iams Nutrition Symposium Proceedings.* Orange Frazer Press.

Reynolds, A., Taylor C., Hoppeler, H., Wiebel, E., Weyand, P., Roberts, T., Reinhart, G. (1996) The Effect of Diet on Sled Dog Performance, Oxidative Capacity, Skeletal Muscle Microstructure, and Muscle Glycogen Metabolism. In *Recent Advances in Canine and Feline Nutrition Volume I: 1996 Iams Nutrition Symposium Proceedings.* Orange Frazer Press.

Water Requirements

Hinchcliff, K., Reinhart, G., Burr, J., Schreier, C., Swenson, R. (1996) Energy Metabolism and Water Turnover in Alaskan Sled Dogs During Running. In *Recent Advances in Canine and Feline Nutrition Volume I: 1996 Iams Nutrition Symposium Proceedings.* Orange Frazer Press.

Reynolds, A. (1993) Water: A Dog's #1 Nutrient. *Mushing.* July/August: 26-28.

Reynolds, A., Sneddon, K., Reinhart, G., Hinchcliff, K., Swenson, R. (1998) Hydration Strategies for Exercising Dogs. In *Recent Advances in Canine and Feline Nutrition Volume II: 1998 Iams Nutrition Symposium Proceedings.* Orange Frazer Press.

JOCELYNN JACOBS

CARL KNOLL